KEYS TO PRODUCTIVE LEADERSHIP

By
ALI KASA

KEYS TO PRODUCTIVE LEADERSHIP

Author: Ali Kasa

Copyright © 2025

All rights reserved. No part of this book may be reproduced or transmitted in any form or by any means, electronic or mechanical, including photocopying, recording, or by an information storage and retrieval system – except by a reviewer who may quote brief passages in a review to be printed in a magazine, newspaper, or on the Web – without permission in writing from the Author.

Edition: Paperback | eBook

DEDICATION

> "Never blame anyone in your life.
> Good people give you happiness.
> Bad people give you experience.
> The worst people give you a lesson.
> And the best people give you memories."
>
> — Zig Ziglar

I look at life as a rollercoaster full of highs, lows, and unexpected turns and I cherish every second of the ride. It has taught me that leadership starts with self-management and is completed only when we engage others and the situation around a shared purpose.

This book is dedicated:

- To the leaders I have worked with,
- To the followers who trusted me,
- And to the future leaders yet to come.

It is also dedicated to every person I have interacted with those who impacted me, and those I hope I have impacted in return.

May we all ride our journey with courage, purpose, and productivity.

— Ali Kasa

TABLE OF CONTENTS

Foreword	1
Part 1: Understanding Leadership	**3**
Chapter 1: Why Another Leadership Book?	7
Chapter 2: Introduction	9
Chapter 3: What Is Leadership?	13
Chapter 4: Leadership Theories	19
Part 2: Focus on the Leader	**25**
Chapter 5: How Does One Starts to be a Leader?	27
Chapter 6: Modes of Influence	31
Chapter 7: The Productive Leader's Framework	37
Chapter 8: The 5Cs of Productive Leadership	45
Chapter 9: Levels of Productive Leadership (John Maxwell Framework)	51
Chapter 10: The Productive Leader	59
Part 3: Focus on the Followers	**67**
Chapter 11: The Productive Follower	71
Chapter 12: The Leader, Follower Model	77
Chapter 13: The Courageous Followers Model	83
Chapter 14: The Productive Follower Growth System	89
Part 4: Focus on the Situation	**97**
Chapter 15: Leading Through Situational Awareness	101
Chapter 16: Assessing Situations	105
Chapter 17: Matching Leadership Style with Situation	111
Chapter 18: Leading in a VUCA World	117
Chapter 19: Situation Engineering	123
Chapter 20: Leading Change	129

Part 5: Tools for Productive Leadership — 135

    Tool 1: The 10 Keys to Productive Leadership Framework — 139
    Tool 2: The Productive Leadership Canvas — 141
    Tool 3: Leader Self-Assessment Diagnostic — 144
    Tool 4: Leadership Style Self-Assessment — 147
    Tool 5: Follower Readiness Questionnaire — 151
    Tool 6: Situation Complexity Questionnaire — 155
    Tool 7: Leadership Style, Situation Matching Grid — 159
    Tool 8: Stress Drivers Diagnostic — 163
    Tool 9: Energy & Presence Tracker — 167
    Tool 10: Values-to-Behavior Alignment Tool — 169
    Tool 11: The 5C Leadership Self-Assessment — 173
    Tool 12: Courageous Follower Assessment — 177
    Tool 13: The Autonomy Spectrum — 181
    Tool 14: VUCA–VUCA Prime Lens — 185
    Tool 15: Change Leadership Roadmap — 189
    Tool 16: Leadership Productivity Scorecard — 193
    Tool 17: Productive Leadership Development Plan — 197

Conclusion: The Keys to Productive Leadership — 201
Final Word from the Author — 205
Epilogue — 207
The Legacy of Leadership — 207
Afterword & Resources — 209
Acknowledgments — 211
Recommended Reading & Inspiration — 213
Books by Ali Kasa — 215
Connect with Ali Kasa — 217
Final Word — 219

FOREWORD

In an age when leadership has become a buzzword and "inspiration" is often mistaken for impact, *Keys to Productive Leadership* brings us back to the essence of what truly matters results through people and purpose.

Leadership today is not a matter of title, charisma, or position. It is a living process a rhythm between leaders, followers, and the situations they face together. It is the discipline of balancing clarity with compassion, vision with adaptability, and purpose with productivity. That is precisely what this book captures so powerfully.

Ali Kasa has built his leadership philosophy on decades of practice not theory. His journey across continents and industries has tested every principle he writes about. From boardrooms and startups to public institutions and community organizations, he has lived what he now shares with us. These pages are not academic reflections; they are a practical blueprint forged in the fires of real leadership.

What makes this book special is its simplicity and depth. It strips away the noise and focuses on what leaders can *do today* how to engage followers, respond to complex situations, and build systems that sustain performance long after the leader is gone. Every chapter is a bridge between knowing and doing, between inspiration and implementation.

As you read, you'll find yourself reflecting, recalibrating, and re-committing not to being "the leader," but to practicing leadership productively. Whether you are a CEO guiding transformation, an entrepreneur building culture, or an emerging professional discovering your potential, the keys you hold in your hands can unlock your most impactful leadership chapter yet.

I invite you to read this book slowly, apply its tools deliberately, and lead with the courage, clarity, and consistency it calls for. Because as Ali reminds us leadership is not who you are; it's what happens between you, your followers, and the world you choose to shape.

PART 1
UNDERSTANDING LEADERSHIP

Part 1: Introduction

Every productive system begins with clarity — and leadership is no different. Before we can talk about followers, situations, or tools, we must first understand the **core process** that makes leadership work.

Most people think of leadership as a trait — something you either have or you don't. Others see it as a position — a title that grants authority. Both views are incomplete. Leadership is not personality, and it is not hierarchy. It is a **relationship in context**: a living exchange between leaders, followers, and the situations they face together.

Part 1 is about resetting that understanding. Here, we dismantle the myths that make leadership mysterious and unproductive. We draw a clear line between **leadership and management**, showing how both are essential but serve different purposes. And we redefine leadership as a **practical, repeatable process** that produces measurable results through others.

You'll explore:

- **What leadership really is** — and why most definitions fail to capture its true nature.
- **How leadership differs from management**, and why organizations need both to perform.
- **The evolution of leadership theories**, from the "great man" era to modern contingency models, and what each contributes to productive practice.
- **A unifying framework** that connects the **leader**, the **Followers**, and the **Situation** — the heart of productive leadership.

Think of this part as your **operating system**. Everything that follows — your personal development as a leader, your relationship with followers, and your ability to navigate complex situations — depends on the clarity you build here.

By the end of Part 1, you'll be able to answer three essential questions with confidence:

- What is leadership, really?
- How do leaders, followers, and situations interact to shape outcomes?
- What makes leadership *productive* rather than reactive or accidental?

Leadership begins with understanding — not inspiration.

Once you grasp its structure, you can practice it deliberately, improve it continuously, and scale it across any organization.

With that clarity, let's begin — by asking the simplest and most important question of all: **What is leadership?**

CHAPTER 1

Why Another Leadership Book?

> *"Leadership is not who you are; it's what happens between leaders, followers, and situations, and the key to productivity is learning to master that process."*
>
> — ALI KASA

Walk into any bookstore or search online, and you'll be flooded with leadership titles. On Amazon alone, there are more than 57,000 leadership books, each promising to unlock the secrets of influence, vision, and success. With so much already written, a fair question arises: why another leadership book?

The answer is simple: most leadership books miss half of the story. They focus almost exclusively on the leader, their charisma, style, and personal traits. While inspiring, this perspective leaves out two critical forces: the followers and the situation. Leadership is not a solo performance. It is a dynamic process where leaders, followers, and context interact to produce outcomes. Ignore one element, and leadership fails.

Too many leaders believe they are born with a fixed style—directive, participative, visionary, or otherwise. They carry this style into every situation as if leadership were a personality trait rather than a discipline. But the most productive leaders are flexible. They understand that style must shift based on the people they are leading and the situation they face. A turnaround crisis demands decisiveness. An innovation sprint calls for empowerment. A new, inexperienced team may need coaching. Leadership is never one-size-fits-all.

PART 1 – UNDERSTANDING LEADERSHIP

Followers, on the other hand, are often treated as passive recipients. Many adopt a victim mentality, believing their role is to simply accept or resist leadership. What they don't realize is that they form 50% of the leadership equation. A leader without engaged followers is just a person with ideas. Followers bring the energy, feedback, accountability, and execution that turn vision into results. Productive leadership emerges when followers step into responsibility, courage, and partnership.

I learned this lesson the hard way. Early in my entrepreneurial journey, I thought my role was to "be the leader", to decide, direct, and push harder. When results lagged, I doubled down with more pressure and more control. But instead of improving, performance deteriorated. My team grew disengaged. Productivity fell. It wasn't until I invited them into the process, listening to their insights, sharing responsibility, and adjusting my style from directive to participative, that momentum returned. Leadership shifted from being about me to being about us.

That's why this book exists. It reframes leadership as a process where leaders, followers, and situations interact in dynamic ways. It gives CEOs, business owners, and professionals the keys to productive leadership: adaptability, empowerment, situational awareness, and practical tools. Each chapter is designed to help you not only understand leadership but practice it productively.

At the end of each chapter, you'll find an exercise or tool. These are not theoretical add-ons; they are frameworks you can use immediately with your teams. For example, in Part 5 you'll find the Productive Leadership Canvas, a one-page map that helps you visualize the leader-follower-situation dynamic in your own organization.

This book is not about becoming a leader in the traditional sense. It's about mastering the process of leadership so you can consistently produce results, build trust with followers, and adapt to a world of constant change.

So why another leadership book? Because leadership isn't just about you. It's about the system you create with others in the situations you face. Once you master that process, leadership becomes not only more productive, but also more meaningful.

CHAPTER 2

Introduction

"Leadership is the capacity to translate vision into reality."

— WARREN BENNIS

Leadership is everywhere. It shapes the way companies grow, the way teams perform, and the way communities thrive. Yet despite its central role in business and society, leadership remains one of the most misunderstood concepts.

Ask ten CEOs to define leadership, and you'll likely get ten different answers. Some will talk about vision, others about influence, others about power. For some, leadership is about charisma; for others, it's about discipline and results. And for too many, leadership is still confused with management.

But here's the truth: management and leadership are not the same thing. Management is about systems, processes, and control. It ensures stability, efficiency, and consistency. Leadership, on the other hand, is about people. It is about creating meaning, direction, and energy. As Peter Drucker once observed, "Management is doing things right; leadership is doing the right things." Both are necessary, but they are not interchangeable.

This confusion is compounded by persistent myths about leadership:

- Leaders are born, not made.
- Leadership is a title or position.
- Followers are powerless.

These myths hold organizations back. They create executives who think they don't need to grow, teams that wait passively for instructions, and cultures that

PART 1 - UNDERSTANDING LEADERSHIP

fail to adapt to change. Leadership is neither a birthright nor a title. Leadership is a process, a dynamic interaction between the leader, the followers, and the situation.

Why does this matter for CEOs, business owners, and professionals today? Because the challenges you face are unlike any in history. Markets shift overnight. Technology reshapes industries. Crises arrive without warning. Followers expect more transparency, engagement, and purpose from leaders. In such an environment, a fixed leadership style is a liability. The leaders who thrive are those who can adapt their style to the situation and bring followers into partnership.

This book is designed as a roadmap to productive leadership. Each part builds on the last:

- **Part 1** sets the foundation by redefining leadership and challenging outdated myths.
- **Part 2** focuses on the leader, your values, vision, and personal attributes.
- **Part 3** shifts the spotlight to followers, the often-ignored half of the leadership equation.
- **Part 4** explores the role of the situation, how context, change, and uncertainty shape leadership choices.
- **Part 5** delivers practical tools, including the Productive Leadership Canvas, that help you put these concepts into action.

At the end of each chapter, you'll find exercises and tools to reflect, assess, and apply what you've learned. These are not theoretical extras; they are practical frameworks you can use immediately with your team.

As you move through this book, I invite you to do three things:

- **Challenge your assumptions** about leadership. Let go of the myth that it is fixed or positional.
- **See yourself as part of a process**, whether you are the leader, the follower, or both at different times.
- **Apply the tools.** Leadership is not learned in theory but in practice, through action, reflection, and adjustment.

The journey ahead is not about becoming a leader in the traditional sense. It is about learning how to lead productively in a way that adapts to change, empowers followers, and delivers results.

This is not just another leadership book. It is a guide to making leadership work in the real world.

CHAPTER 3

What Is Leadership?

Leadership is not a title you hold, but a process you practice, a dynamic exchange between leaders, followers, and situations."

— ALI KASA

Leadership is one of the most discussed and least understood disciplines in the world of work. We teach it in classrooms, demand it from managers, and celebrate it in biographies—yet most organizations still struggle to describe what effective leadership truly looks like.

The confusion often comes from treating leadership as an **identity** instead of a **process**. Many believe leaders are born, or that charisma, authority, or seniority automatically make someone effective. In reality, leadership is neither a personality trait nor a position. It is a **series of actions** that align people toward a shared purpose, regardless of hierarchy.

This part of the book lays the groundwork. Before we can talk about tools or systems, we must ask:

- What is leadership?
- How is it different from management?
- Why do so many myths cloud our understanding?
- And how can leaders shift from instinct or charisma to a more deliberate, productive approach?

PART 1 - UNDERSTANDING LEADERSHIP

By clarifying these fundamentals, we prepare the ground for everything that follows. Leadership may take many forms, but at its core, it is always a **relationship in context**.

In my own journey, I went through phases of hunger, confusion, and validation before I found clarity. At first, I devoured leadership books, hungry to understand the secret of influence. Soon, I found myself confused: the books contradicted one another, was leadership charisma, strategy, or discipline? My validation came not from theory but from practice. In business and community roles, I failed at times and succeeded at others. What I learned was simple but profound: leadership is not who you are; it's what you do with others in the situations you face.

So what is leadership?

Leadership is the process of recognizing responsibility, choosing the right mode of influence, and working with followers in each situation to achieve a productive outcome that would not have been possible otherwise.

Breaking it down further:

- The **Leader** provides vision, values, energy, and direction.
- The **Followers** contribute motivation, feedback, and accountability.
- The **Situation** dictates which leadership style will work best.
- The **Mode of Influence**, whether directing, coaching, empowering, or inspiring, connects the leader and followers.
- The **Outcome** is the ultimate measure of leadership, because results matter.

This process is easier to grasp when visualized.

The Leadership Process Diagram

As shown in the diagram below, leadership can be understood as a simple but powerful equation:

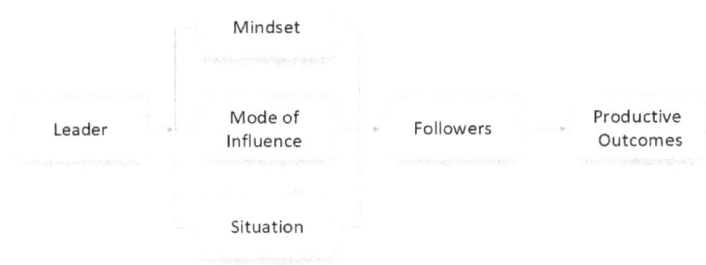

Figure 1: The Productive Leadership Model

This reminds us that leadership is not a static trait or title. It is the dynamic interaction of these three forces, connected through influence, and measured by results.

Leadership vs. Management

It's important to separate leadership from management. Management is about systems, order, and control. Leadership is about direction, meaning, and influence. Management ensures that things are done right. Leadership ensures that the right things are done. A business needs both, but they are not the same. The diagram below illustrates how leadership is different from management and at the same time it shows that both contribute to achievements of same goals and complement each other.

Figure 2: Leadership Vs. Management

PART 1 - UNDERSTANDING LEADERSHIP

Adaptability and Situations

Another key insight is that leadership is situational. You may have a natural style, directive, participative, or visionary, but no single style works in every context. A start-up in crisis demands decisiveness; a mature organization may require collaboration; a high-performing team thrives with empowerment. Productive leaders are adaptable, switching styles as situations change.

Case Study 1
Tony Fernandes and the Rebirth of AirAsia

In 2001, entrepreneur **Tony Fernandes** made a daring move: he purchased a failing Malaysian airline, AirAsia, for just one ringgit (about $0.25) and assumed approximately $11 million in debt. At the time, the airline had just two aging planes and little hope of turning profitable.

Fernandes had little aviation experience. What he brought instead was vision, humility, and belief, but above all, a different understanding of leadership. He famously staked everything, mortgaging his home, to ask, **"Why can't air travel be affordable to everyone?"** That became AirAsia's rallying cry: *"Now, everyone can fly."*

Fernandes' leadership approach was a blend of **Democratic, Charismatic, and Servant leadership**:

- He **empowered** his team by breaking hierarchical norms, any employee could walk into his office with an idea or a problem.
- He **role-modeled accessibility and openness**, championed ideas from the frontline, and treated employees like partners, not subordinates.
- He **inspired** by aligning vision with deep cultural change, persuading thousands to believe in AirAsia's shared mission.

Within two years, AirAsia turned profitable. Fernandes instituted fierce cost controls, from single aircraft models to digital ticketing, while reinforcing a culture of trust, energy, and ownership.

KEYS TO PRODUCTIVE LEADERSHIP

Under his leadership, the airline expanded rapidly to serve over 65 cities by 2006, and today it spans more than 166 destinations across the Asia-Pacific.

What this tells us:

Fernandes succeeded not by asserting authority, but by **creating space for meaningful collaboration between leader, followers, and situation**. He adapted his style to the context and nurtured productivity, not by forcing compliance, but by aligning vision, engaging people, and simplifying structures.

This case clearly shows that **leadership is a process**, and that great productivity often comes from humility, trust, and alignment, not titles or force.

Exercise 1: Reflect on Your Leadership Process

Think of a recent leadership situation where you had to work with your team. Reflect and write your thoughts below:

1. Did I recognize the role I was playing as a leader?

_____

_____

2. Did I choose the right mode of influence for my followers and the situation?

_____

_____

3. Did the outcome reflect productivity, or could it have been better with a different approach?

_____

_____

For a structured way to analyze this, use the Productive Leadership Canvas in Part 5. It helps you map the leader, followers, situation, purpose, systems and outcomes on one page to see where the gaps are.

CHAPTER 4

Leadership Theories

"Leadership and learning are indispensable to each other."

— JOHN F. KENNEDY

A theory is a way of explaining the patterns we observe in the world. It offers a lens for understanding complex human behavior and predicting outcomes. In leadership, theories help us interpret what makes people follow, why some leaders succeed in one context and fail in another, and how influence actually works. Each theory reveals part of the truth, but none alone captures the full picture.

Over time, leadership thinking has evolved—from the belief that leaders are born to the understanding that leadership can be learned, practiced, and adapted. The following overview traces this progression and highlights what each perspective contributes to **productive leadership**.

The Great Man Theory

One of the earliest approaches proposed that leaders are born, not made, and that history is shaped by extraordinary individuals who naturally rise to power.

History and modern experience challenge this notion. As Singapore's founding prime minister **Lee Kuan Yew** observed, "One may be born with some leadership qualities, but that alone is not sufficient to be a great one." The Great Man Theory's value lies in recognizing that personal qualities matter; its limitation is that it discourages development. Leadership becomes destiny rather than discipline.

Trait Theories

Building on that foundation, trait theories sought to identify characteristics common among effective leaders—qualities such as intelligence, confidence, decisiveness, and charisma.

Research confirmed that these traits influence success, yet traits alone do not guarantee great leadership. They are the raw material. Without the right behaviors, followers, and context, traits remain potential rather than productivity.

Behavioral Theories

By the mid-twentieth century, attention shifted from *who leaders are* to *what leaders do*. Behavioral theories emphasized observable actions and styles—democratic, autocratic, task-focused, or people-focused.

This shift was transformative because it proved that leadership can be taught and practiced. **Jack Welch** at General Electric demonstrated a results-driven approach that emphasized clarity and accountability, while **Herb Kelleher** at Southwest Airlines modeled a people-centered style that built loyalty and culture. Each achieved productivity through different behavioral focus. Still, no single behavior works in every context.

Situational and Contingency Theories

As understanding matured, scholars recognized that behavior must fit the situation. Situational leadership theory argues that the best style depends on the readiness of followers and the surrounding circumstances: sometimes leaders must direct; at other times they should coach, support, or delegate.

Contingency theories expanded this idea, linking effectiveness to task complexity, environment, and team dynamics. Dwight Eisenhower, who led the Allied invasion of Europe in World War II, exemplified this flexibility—adapting his approach with politicians, generals, and soldiers alike. Adaptability, not personality, became the hallmark of effective leadership.

Transactional Leadership

Transactional leadership views the leader–follower relationship as an exchange: performance is rewarded and failure corrected. It provides structure, clarity, and accountability—qualities especially valuable in disciplined or high-risk settings such as the military or large corporations.

However, transactions create compliance more than commitment. They maintain order but rarely spark innovation or purpose.

Transformational Leadership

Transformational leadership moves beyond transactions to vision, inspiration, and empowerment. Transformational leaders ignite passion and purpose, lifting followers beyond self-interest toward shared goals.

Steve Jobs challenged his teams to "think different," while **Mother Teresa** modeled compassion that mobilized thousands. Transformational leadership can change cultures and organizations—but even this style requires engaged followers and a supportive situation to succeed.

What We Learn from Theories

Each perspective contributes a vital lesson:

- **Great Man Theory** – Personal qualities influence impact but don't guarantee it.
- **Trait Theories** – Attributes matter only when applied productively.
- **Behavioral Theories** – Leadership can be learned and practiced.
- **Situational and Contingency Theories** – Adaptability is essential.
- **Transactional Leadership** – Ensures accountability and structure.
- **Transformational Leadership** – Inspires purpose and passion.

No single theory is sufficient. Leadership is a process—the alignment of leader, followers, and situation. Theories are not rules but tools. The productive leader draws from all of them, applying what fits the people and the context.

Case Study 2
Jack Ma and the Rise of Alibaba

Jack Ma, once an English teacher rejected from dozens of jobs, founded Alibaba Group in 1999 to connect small Chinese businesses with global markets. Within five years he outmaneuvered eBay's entry into China through Taobao's customer-first strategy. By 2014 Alibaba's IPO raised US $25 billion—the largest in history—and the company grew into a global ecosystem employing more than 200,000 people.

Leadership Insights

- **Transformational Dimension** – Ma painted a compelling vision and empowered employees to innovate and take ownership of that vision.
- **Charismatic Dimension** – His authentic storytelling and optimism built emotional connection and resilience during rapid growth.

Together these dimensions disprove the "born leader" myth and demonstrate that leadership is crafted through purpose, presence, and adaptability.

Exercise 2: Applying Theories in Practice

Think about a leadership challenge you faced recently. Which theory best describes your approach? Write down your reflections below:

1. Which theory did I naturally use?

_____

_____

2. Did it fit the situation and the followers?

_____

_____

3. What different approach might have produced a better outcome?

_____

_____

For practical guidance, see the **Style Matching Grid** in Part 5. It will help you align your leadership approach with the demands of the situation.

No single theory defines leadership. Each explains one dimension of a larger system. Productive leadership blends them—adapting traits, behaviors, and influence to fit followers and context. Understanding these foundations prepares you for **Part 2: Focus on the Leader**, where we explore the inner architecture of leadership—the values, character, and habits that make every theory work in practice.

Part 1: Summary

Part 1 redefines leadership as a process rather than a position. It begins by dismantling the myths that leadership is innate or reserved for those with authority, showing instead that leadership is a learnable, repeatable discipline built on clarity, purpose, and adaptability.

We explored how productive leadership emerges from the dynamic relationship between **the leader, the Followers, and the situation**—a system where effectiveness depends on alignment and fit. Leadership becomes productive when influence matches follower readiness and contextual demands.

The distinction between **leadership and management** clarified that both are essential: management sustains systems; leadership mobilizes people. Together they turn vision into execution.

Finally, by examining major **leadership theories**, we traced the evolution from traits and behaviors to adaptability and transformation. Each theory contributes a tool, but none alone defines success.

The key takeaway:

Productive leadership is contextual, relational, and deliberate. It thrives when leaders act with purpose, engage followers as partners, and adapt their approach to the realities of the moment. This understanding forms the foundation for everything that follows—beginning with **Part 2: Focus on the Leader.**

PART 2
FOCUS ON THE LEADER

Part 2: Introduction

Leadership begins within. Before a person can inspire others, they must first learn to lead themselves — to manage their mindset, master their emotions, and align their actions with purpose. Part 2 explores this inner architecture of leadership — the beliefs, values, disciplines, and habits that form the core of every productive leader.

In Part 1, we established that leadership is a process — a dynamic relationship between the **Leader**, the **Followers**, and the **Situation**. This part now zooms in on the first element of that process: **the Leader**. The foundation of all productive leadership lies in who the leader is — not in title or charisma, but in **character, competence, courage, and clarity of purpose**.

Here, you'll explore what shapes a leader from the inside out:

- **How leaders are made**, not born — through growth, reflection, and practice.
- **The building blocks of leadership**, including power, values, vision, and focus.
- **The 5 Cs of Leadership** — Character, Competence, Communication, Courage, and Care — and how they define credibility.
- **The levels and styles of influence**, showing how leaders evolve as they gain trust and responsibility.

Every chapter in this section is designed to help you turn awareness into action. You'll be challenged to reflect on your personal journey, test your leadership DNA, and strengthen the principles that guide your decisions.

Before you can lead others, you must master the person you bring into every situation — yourself.

This is where productive leadership truly begins. Let's step inward and explore what it means to become the kind of leader others choose to follow.

CHAPTER 5

How Does One Starts to be a Leader?

"Before you are a leader, success is all about growing yourself. When you become a leader, success is all about growing others."

— JACK WELCH

The Leader in the Productive Leadership Model

In the **Productive Leadership Model**, the *Leader* is the anchor of the entire system. While the *Followers* bring energy and the *Situation* brings complexity, it is the *Leader* who integrates both into purposeful action. The leader sets the tone, rhythm, and moral compass of productivity — translating vision into behavior, and behavior into measurable results. When the leader is aligned, the system functions with clarity and coherence; when the leader is fragmented, even capable followers and favorable situations lose direction. Leadership productivity, therefore, begins not with authority but with **self-regulation** — the ability to manage one's mindset, choices, and energy so that others can align confidently. The leader's greatest responsibility is not to control people, but to **create conditions where others perform at their best**.

The Productive Leadership Mindset

Mindset is the foundation of productive leadership — the inner framework that shapes how a leader thinks, perceives, and responds. It governs what information they notice, how they interpret it, and which choices they ultimately make. A *productive mindset* is anchored in purpose, curiosity, and responsibility. It seeks to understand before judging, to learn before reacting, and to act with clarity rather than emotion. Every productive outcome begins not with action, but with awareness.

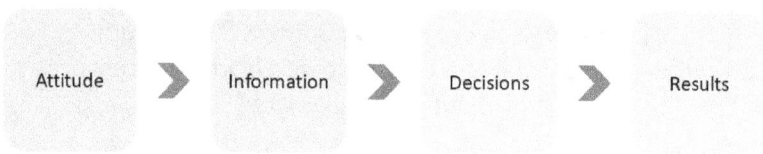

Figure 3: Decision Making Model

As illustrated in **Figure 3**, results are the visible end of an invisible sequence: first comes the *mindset*, which determines the *information* a leader collects and trusts; accurate and complete information enables sound *decisions*; and effective decisions produce sustainable *results*. When a leader adjusts their mindset, they transform the quality of information they receive, the wisdom of their decisions, and the productivity of their results.

How Leadership Starts

Leadership does not begin with appointment or ambition; it begins with awareness. While skills can be taught, the *capacity for leadership* exists in every human being. **Ali Kasa** believes that people are born with a basic leadership framework — the natural ability to influence, decide, and act. The responsibility of parents and early educators is to nurture this foundation by teaching **self-management**, discipline, and emotional control. This is the first true step in *productive leadership*: the ability to **lead oneself**. The ancient maxim applies perfectly — *"you cannot give what you do not have."* A leader who cannot manage their own thoughts, energy, and emotions cannot expect to guide others productively.

KEYS TO PRODUCTIVE LEADERSHIP

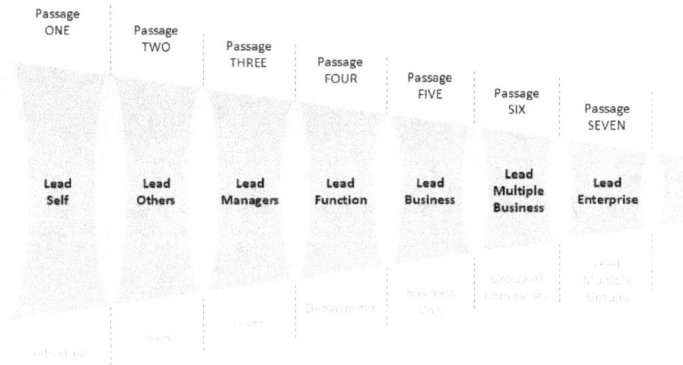

Figure 4: The Drotter & Charan Leadership Pipeline Model

As illustrated in Figure 4: The Leadership Pipeline, leadership growth follows a progressive flow — from Leading Self to Leading Others, Leading Managers, Leading Functions, Leading Businesses, and finally Leading the Enterprise. Each transition demands new competencies, new perspectives, and, most importantly, a renewed mindset. Every higher level of leadership begins with mastering the level below — and it all starts with the disciplined art of self-leadership.

Personal Story

It was just after 5:30 p.m. in Kuala Lumpur, Malaysia, sometime in 2003—the height of rush hour—when a sudden downpour flooded the streets and paralyzed traffic. The signal lights had malfunctioned, rain pounded against windshields, and frustrated drivers leaned on their horns, trapped in a sea of motionless cars. I sat there watching the chaos unfold, each person waiting for someone else to fix the problem.

Then, out of nowhere, an old man—drenched, barefoot, and holding a torn plastic bag above his head—stepped into the middle of the intersection. With nothing but his hands and quiet determination, he began directing the traffic. Left hand up, right hand forward—firm, calm, and precise. Within minutes, the vehicles started to move again. Order replaced confusion. The man had no title, no uniform, and no authority. He simply saw a problem and acted.

When I rolled down my window and thanked him, he smiled and said words I will never forget:

PART 2 - FOCUS ON THE LEADER

"You don't need permission or position to lead—only the opportunity."

That moment reshaped my understanding of leadership. It revealed that leadership begins when a person chooses responsibility over comfort and action over hesitation. It doesn't wait for power; it responds to purpose. The story embodies the core of *productive leadership*—leadership starts when mindset meets opportunity, and initiative turns chaos into progress.

Exercise 3: Leading Self Audit

1. Where in your current role or environment can you take initiative without waiting for permission?
   _____
   _____

2. What habits strengthen or weaken your ability to lead yourself?
   _____
   _____

3. What one behavior could you change today to increase your personal productivity and influence?
   _____
   _____

Repeat this self-audit quarterly. Leadership begins the moment you measure and manage yourself deliberately.

Leadership begins within. The *leader* in the **productive leadership model** is the organizing force that aligns followers and situations through clarity, courage, and care. A productive leader cultivates the right **mindset**, which shapes the **information** they trust, the **decisions** they make, and the **results** they deliver. Leadership does not start with position but with purpose—the readiness to lead oneself before leading others. From the flooded intersection in Kuala Lumpur to the structured transitions of the **Leadership Pipeline**, the message is constant: when mindset, responsibility, and opportunity meet, leadership is born.

CHAPTER 6
Modes of Influence

"Leadership is influence—nothing more, nothing less."

— JOHN C. MAXWELL

Leadership is influence—the ability to move people toward a shared purpose through trust, clarity, and conviction. In the Productive Leadership Model, influence is the point where the leader's mindset interacts with followers and the situation to produce results.

Many leaders proudly say, "I lead by example." While this reflects integrity, it represents only one dimension of influence—modeling behavior. Productive leaders go further: they understand how to adapt their influence to what the situation and people require. Influence is therefore a mindset in motion—the translation of thought into behavior and behavior into results.

The Mindset Primer

Influence begins in the leader's mind. The productive leader first asks, "What mindset does this situation require from me?" The right mindset determines the right mode of influence. Rigid leaders apply the same approach everywhere; productive leaders read the context and respond intentionally. Influence is not about style preference—it's about situational precision. Leadership influence exists on a continuum, not as a single method or identity. This continuum is captured in the Productive Influence Spectrum.

PART 2 - FOCUS ON THE LEADER

The Productive Influence Spectrum

Leadership influence operates on a spectrum rather than a single style. Productive leaders understand that people and situations evolve, so influence must evolve too. At one end of the spectrum, leaders provide clarity and direction; at the other, they develop others through trust and coaching. Between these points lie distinct modes of influence that reflect different leadership mindsets—from enforcing structure to empowering autonomy and nurturing growth.

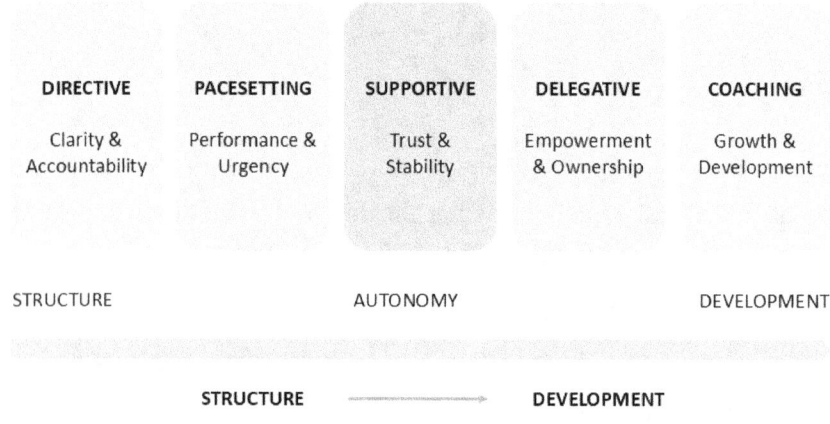

Figure 5: The Productive Influence Spectrum

As illustrated in **Figure 5,** the spectrum flows from Directive (Clarity & Accountability) to Pacesetting (Performance & Urgency), Supportive (Trust & Stability), Delegative (Empowerment & Ownership), and finally Coaching (Growth & Development). This progression mirrors the natural journey of leadership maturity: moving from control to collaboration to cultivation. Productive leaders learn to shift fluidly across this range, choosing the mode that best fits their followers' readiness and the situation's demands. The ability to adapt influence—rather than rely on habit—transforms leadership from personality into purposeful productivity.

Figure 5 illustrates how leaders shift intentionally between modes of influence—from structure to empowerment to development—according to mindset, follower readiness, and situational demands.

The Five Modes of Productive Influence

Directive Mode

When direction is unclear or speed is essential, the leader provides structure, clarity, and standards. The mindset is: "**My role is to define what good looks like and set the path forward.**" Directive influence is most productive during crisis, change, or inexperience. It provides safety through certainty. Yet, when overused, it can create dependency—followers wait instead of act.

Pacesetting Mode

The pacesetting leader leads by example—setting the standard through their own work ethic and results. The mindset is "I **drive performance by demonstrating excellence.**" This mode creates momentum in competent, motivated teams but can lead to fatigue or burnout if overused.

Supportive Mode

Supportive leaders focus on emotional climate. They create stability when change, stress, or fatigue threatens morale. The mindset is: "**My presence should reduce fear and increase confidence.**" This mode is especially valuable in uncertainty, transition, or recovery periods.

Delegative Mode

Delegation reflects trust. It transfers responsibility and decision-making authority to capable followers. The mindset is "I **trust you to decide, act, and deliver.**" Delegation builds autonomy, confidence, and leadership maturity.

Coaching Mode

The coaching leader believes success is measured by how many others grow. The mindset is: "**I develop people so that they can perform and lead without me.**" This mode is used when the goal is capability, not just compliance.

The Productive Influence Comparison Table

Mode	Core Mindset	When It's Productive	Risk if overused
Directive	Clarity & Accountability	Crisis, new teams, urgent delivery	Dependency, low creativity
Pacesetting	Performance & Urgency	Skilled teams, high standard goals	Burnout, disengagement
Supportive	Trust & Stability	Change fatigue, low morale	Complacency, low challenge
Delegative	Empowerment & Ownership	Mature, capable teams	Drift, loss of alignment
Coaching	Growth & Development	Building capability, long-term success	Slow speed, over-analysis

Adapting Your Mode of Influence

Influence is dynamic. Productive leaders move intentionally across the spectrum depending on who they lead and what the situation requires. When followers are new, directive influence brings structure. When they are competent, delegation builds confidence. When they are demotivated, supportive or inspirational influence reignites energy. Rigid leaders apply one mode everywhere; adaptive leaders read the moment and respond accordingly. Productive leaders lead with intention, not habit.

Personal Story

My natural style is **pacesetting.** I work hard, set high standards, and expect my team to match my drive. But one day, I noticed that my team was not catching up with me. I asked, and when I pressed them on why they weren't keeping pace, their answer was blunt: "We are exhausted. We don't have the same motivations as you."

That moment shifted me. I realized that while pacesetting helped me achieve results, it was burning out my team. I was stuck in **Level 3 (Production),** driving outcomes but failing to grow into **Level 4 (People Development).** Since then, I've made a conscious effort to balance pacesetting with **coaching** and **affiliative** styles, ensuring results come without sacrificing energy or growth.

Exercise 4: Identify Your Dominant Mode of Influence

1. Which mode of influence do you use most naturally, and why?

_____

_____

2. Which mode do you underuse? What mindset might limit your flexibility?

_____

_____

3. Reflect on a recent challenge: how might a different influence mode have produced a better result?

_____

_____

Ask your team which mode they experience most from you—their perception often reveals the gap between intent and impact.

Influence is the behavioral expression of mindset. When leaders adjust their mindset, their mode of influence shifts—and so do their results. Productive leadership is not about having one style; it is about understanding people, purpose, and context and responding with the right influence at the right time. In the Productive Leadership Model, influence is the bridge that connects mindset to measurable results—where leadership becomes both visible and valuable.

CHAPTER 7

The Productive Leader's Framework

"The foundation of leadership is not power, but purpose — the ability to build systems that outlast you."

— PETER DRUCKER

Leadership as Architecture

Leadership, like architecture, is an act of deliberate construction. Vision gives a leader direction, and influence moves people toward it, *but only structure makes both endure.* Every great leader builds something: a company, a culture, or a cause. What differentiates the productive leader is not what they achieve in moments of inspiration, but what remains when they are no longer present.

In the **Productive Leadership Model**, this process begins with *mindset*, shaped by *information*, expressed through *decisions*, and measured by results. The leader's mindset becomes visible through the systems they design and the culture they sustain.

The **Productive Leadership Canvas** (see Part 5, Tool 2) translates these ideas into action. It visualizes leadership as a living framework—made of purpose, power, values, vision, focus, systems, traits & behaviors, results, personality & intelligence, and energy & magnetism. Each element interacts with the others, forming a complete structure for sustainable leadership. As you move through this chapter, imagine sketching your own canvas—a blueprint for how you intend to lead and live.

PART 2 - FOCUS ON THE LEADER

The Productive Leader's Framework

The Productive Leader's Framework illustrates how effective leadership integrates being and doing. At the center lies the **leader,** built on four foundations—purpose, **values, traits & behaviors, and energy & magnetism.** These inner qualities define identity, integrity, and inspiration.

Surrounding the core is the **Outer System** of leadership—Vision, **Focus, Systems, and Results**—where mindset turns into measurable impact. Connecting both layers are **power & influence** and **personality & intelligence,** bridging intention and execution.

This model demonstrates that productive leadership is a cycle—Mindset → **Information** → **Decision** → **Results**—linking self-awareness to sustainable performance. It reminds us that leadership is not a title or moment, but a continuous system of purpose, clarity, and results.

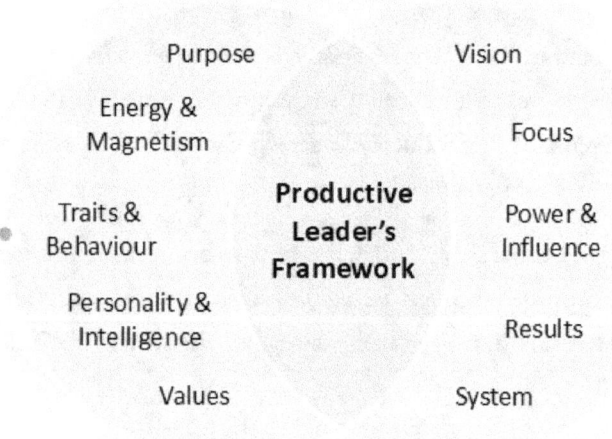

Figure 6: The Productive Leader's Framework

With the framework in view, we now explore each building block in depth. Each represents a structural layer of leadership—from inner purpose to outer results—that together forms a complete and resilient design.

1. Purpose – The Anchor of Leadership

Purpose is the starting point of all productive leadership. It answers *why* a leader exists—not to manage tasks, but to create meaning. Purpose turns ambition into direction and struggle into strength.

Leaders without purpose drift between opportunities; leaders with purpose align every decision, relationship, and resource toward a greater cause. Purpose transforms power from control into contribution.

In the **Leadership Canvas**, Purpose sits at the center — influencing how leaders think, act, and build. Without a clear "why," the building blocks of leadership may stand, but they cannot hold. Purpose gives leadership moral direction before strategic direction.

2. Power & Influence – The Engine of Leadership

Power is the ability to cause movement; **influence** is the art of doing so willingly. Power compels; influence inspires. The productive leader learns to use power responsibly, aware that authority may grant obedience but only integrity earns trust.

Mahatma Gandhi influenced millions without formal authority. **Angela Merkel** led through credibility and calm. **Elon Musk**, though controversial, demonstrates how vision-based power can mobilize industries.

In productive leadership, power and influence must be anchored in purpose — directed toward value creation, not self-promotion.

3. Values – The Compass of Leadership

Values are the moral architecture that holds leadership together. They define what is acceptable, honorable, and non-negotiable.

Leaders like **Howard Schultz** of Starbucks or **Muhammad Ali** demonstrated that strong values generate trust — not through speeches, but through sacrifice. When values and actions align, credibility becomes currency.

In the **Productive Leadership Model**, values are filters through which decisions pass. They ensure that results never outpace integrity.

4. Vision – The Horizon of Leadership

Vision is leadership's long-range view. It defines what does not yet exist but must. Vision transforms the leader's purpose into a collective dream others can see and believe in.

Steve Jobs once said, *"You have to be burning with an idea, or a problem, or a wrong that you want to right."* Vision is that fire. Yet, vision without focus is imagination; *focus turns vision into motion.*

5. Focus—The Discipline of Leadership

Focus is the leader's ability to align attention with intention. It means saying *no* to distractions that dilute energy. Productive leaders understand that clarity is kind—to themselves and others.

When Jobs returned to Apple, he eliminated dozens of products to focus on four. That discipline birthed the iMac, iPhone, and iPad. Focus channels effort into impact; it transforms scattered movement into productive progress. In my experience, structure does not limit leadership; it liberates it.

But focus alone is not enough—it must be reinforced by systems that make clarity operational.

6. Systems—The Architecture of Productivity

Systems are how leadership becomes sustainable. They are the structures, routines, and rhythms that turn values and focus into measurable outcomes. Where purpose gives direction and focus sets priorities, *systems create consistency.*

Dr. W. Edwards Deming said, "A bad system will beat a good person every time."

Productive leaders build systems that enable ordinary people to deliver extraordinary results—not through constant supervision but through clarity and design. In the **Leadership Canvas**, systems connect purpose, vision, and results. They ensure that leadership is measurable, repeatable, and resilient.

7. Traits & Behaviors – The Practice of Leadership

Traits are the inner capacities of a leader; behaviors are how those capacities manifest. Traits define *who you are*; behaviors define *how you show up*. Courage, empathy, discipline, and resilience are productive traits. Listening, delegating, deciding, and learning are productive behaviors. Together, they form the habit of leadership.

Productive leaders don't rely on talent; they refine behavior until it becomes instinct.

8. Results—The Proof of Leadership

Results are the visible outcomes of invisible leadership. They validate the system, the discipline, and the purpose. In productive leadership, results are not about personal recognition but about collective performance.

Leaders who focus only on metrics lose meaning; those who connect metrics to purpose multiply impact. Results are proof that the architecture of leadership works. Results without reflection become repetition.

9. Personality & Intelligence—The Tools of Leadership

Intelligence enables leaders to understand complexity; personality allows them to connect emotionally. One without the other produces imbalance—the brilliant but cold strategist or the kind but ineffective manager.

Satya Nadella's transformation of Microsoft, combining empathy with innovation, illustrates emotional intelligence at work. Productive leadership demands both clarity of thought and authenticity of presence.

10. Energy & Magnetism – The Aura of Leadership

Energy is leadership's invisible currency. It determines how long and how deeply a leader can sustain impact. Magnetism is energy expressed through presence—it draws others into purpose.

When purpose and systems align, leaders generate energy instead of consuming it. Their presence becomes a source of clarity, courage, and calm.

This magnetic energy enables leaders to operate at the inspirational end of the *Productive Influence Spectrum* (Chapter 6).

PART 2 - FOCUS ON THE LEADER

Case Study 3
Ratan Tata – Building with Purpose and Systems

Few leaders embody the building blocks of leadership like **Ratan Tata.** His purpose—improving the quality of life for Indians—defined his leadership decisions for decades. Guided by values of humility and national service, Tata infused vision into every enterprise—from steel and automobiles to philanthropy and technology.

When he launched the Tata Nano, it wasn't just about creating a low-cost car; it was about giving dignity to families who could only afford a scooter. His leadership blended empathy with systems—a structure that allowed thousands of employees to align around a social vision.

Tata's enduring legacy lies not only in profits but also in principles. He built companies that became instruments of progress—systems of purpose that outlasted him.

Exercise 5—Designing Your Productive Leader's Framework

Review the *Leadership Canvas (Part 5, Tool 2)* and the Productive Leader's Framework.

1. Identify which of the ten building blocks are strongest for you.

_____

_____

2. Which one or two need the most reinforcement?

_____

_____

3. How does your *purpose* currently align with your *systems*?

_____

_____

3. Write one action you will take this month to strengthen your weakest block.

_____

_____

4. Sketch how your ten blocks connect—is there a gap between vision and results or purpose and energy?

_____

_____

A strong framework balances the inner world (purpose, values, traits, and energy) with the outer world (vision, focus, systems, and results).

Leadership is not built in a day; it is built in layers. Purpose anchors direction. Power moves people. Values define boundaries. Vision gives form. Focus sharpens effort. Systems sustain consistency. Traits and behaviors reinforce character. Results validate structure. Personality and intelligence give texture. Energy gives life.

Together, these ten building blocks create *leadership architecture*—a framework that transforms mindset into movement and movement into meaning. As **Peter Drucker** said, the true test of leadership is not what happens when you are present, but what continues when you are gone.

CHAPTER 8
The 5Cs of Productive Leadership

"Leadership is a matter of how to be, not how to do."
— FRANCES HESSELBEIN

Leadership excellence is not born from technique but from temperament. The *5Cs of Productive Leadership* — **Character, Competence, Communication, Courage, and Care** — form the behavioral architecture of leadership. They define *how a leader shows up*, not just *what a leader does*.

In the *Productive Leadership Model*, mindset drives behavior, and behavior sustains culture. These five Cs act as the bridge between *purpose* (the inner world of the leader) and *results* (the outer world of the organization). They serve as both a **mirror** and a **map**:

- A *mirror* for self-reflection—revealing strengths and blind spots.
- A *map* for direction—guiding followers on what to expect from those they choose to follow.

The *Productive Leadership Canvas* (Part 5, Tool 2) embeds the 5Cs as behavioral checkpoints that ensure alignment between *values, systems,* and *results.*

1. Character—The Core of Trust

Every system of leadership collapses without trust. Trust begins where *character* is visible—in the alignment between values, words, and actions.

Character is not situational; it is consistent under pressure. It's how leaders behave when no one is watching and when everyone is watching.

Productive leaders translate Purpose into Character. They hold to integrity when it costs them, because they understand that leadership measured by convenience is not leadership—it's performance.

Reflection: *Do I live by my values even when they cost me?*

2. Competence—The Foundation of Credibility

Competence gives leadership substance. It's the ability to understand, decide, and deliver. Followers expect leaders to master their craft—not to know everything, but to learn continually. Competence is how *vision* becomes *results*.

When **Satya Nadella** took over Microsoft, his focus on cloud transformation and AI repositioned the company for the future. His competence lay not only in technology but also in foresight and empathy—knowing both what to do and how to do it with people.

Within the *Productive Leader's Framework*, competence is where *knowledge meets impact*.

Reflection: *Am I continuously upgrading my capability to lead with clarity and deliver with excellence?*

3. Communication—The Channel of Alignment

Leadership lives or dies in communication. It's how clarity travels, conflict dissolves, and culture takes shape.

Communication is not just the ability to speak—it's the discipline to listen, translate complexity into simplicity, and ensure everyone walks away aligned.

Jacinda Ardern demonstrated this during New Zealand's toughest moments. Her empathy didn't dilute authority; it amplified it. She showed that tone is part of strategy—and that words, when used with care, can heal, not just inform.

In the *Productive Leadership Canvas*, communication links Purpose to People. It converts conviction into collective understanding.

Reflection: *Do I listen deeply enough for others to feel heard, and do my words bring clarity or confusion?*

4. Courage—The Catalyst for Change

Courage is the defining test of leadership. It means doing what's right when silence is safer and choosing principle over popularity.

Every major transformation—personal or organizational—begins with a courageous decision.

Muhammad Ali's refusal to fight in Vietnam was not defiance; it was conviction. His courage cost him his titles but won him moral authority that endures beyond sport. Productive leaders align courage with purpose. They face reality, challenge inertia, and protect values—even when the path forward is uncertain.

Reflection: *Do I confront uncomfortable truths, or do I compromise to maintain comfort?*

5. Care—The Heart of Leadership

Care transforms leadership from positional power into personal stewardship. It's how leaders connect humanity to performance.

Followers commit when they feel seen, respected, and supported—not as resources, but as people with potential.

Herb Kelleher of Southwest Airlines embodied this truth. His care for employees created an enduring culture of loyalty and innovation. Productive leaders understand that *care* fuels *energy—the* force that sustains teams through change and challenge.

In the *Productive Leader's Framework*, care is the emotional infrastructure that binds systems to people and values to results.

Reflection: *Do the people I lead feel valued, developed, and genuinely cared for under my leadership?*

Integrating the 5Cs

The 5Cs are not isolated virtues—they are interdependent forces within the *Productive Leadership Model.*

- **Character** builds *trust*—the foundation of all influence.
- **Competence** builds *credibility*—the foundation of results.
- **Communication** builds *connection*—the foundation of culture.
- **Courage** builds *change*—the foundation of progress.
- **Care** builds *commitment*—the foundation of belonging.

When integrated, the 5Cs align *who the leader is* with *how the leader leads.* They turn leadership from performance into presence, from control into contribution, and from management into meaning.

Personal Story – Discovering My 5C Blind Spots

In 2008, I invited a leadership coach to help my team and me perform at our best. She conducted a survey asking my team to rate me across the 5Cs. The results surprised me—my lowest score was **Communication.**

I realized I was leading with intensity but not always with attentiveness. My fast pace—my "hurry-up" nature—sometimes made me appear impatient or unavailable. Though unintentional, it created distance.

That experience became a turning point. Since then, I've repeated the 5C assessment annually. It's not just a tool—it's a mirror. It reminds me that leadership maturity is measured not by how we see ourselves, but by how those we serve experience us.

This ritual became part of my *Productive Leadership System*—a loop of self-awareness, feedback, and growth.

Exercise 6: Self-Reflection

Rate yourself on a scale of 1 (rarely) to 5 (always) for each C:

Leadership Dimension	Description	Rating (1–5)
Character	Integrity, honesty, and follow-through	___
Competence	Skill mastery, judgment, and results	___
Communication	Listening, clarity, and feedback	___
Courage	Principled action, risk-taking, and conviction	___
Care	Empathy, respect, and development of others	___

Reflection Prompts:

1. Which C represents your strongest foundation?

_____

_____

2. Which one requires your greatest attention and growth?

_____

_____

3. How will you apply your self-insight to strengthen your team's trust and performance?

_____

_____

4. How will you invite feedback to test your perception against reality?

_____

_____

PART 2 - FOCUS ON THE LEADER

Part 5 includes a 5Cs Leadership Feedback Template you can use immediately.

The 5Cs of Productive Leadership form the behavioral code of the *Productive Leader's Model*. They shape how leaders think, act, and connect — ensuring that every decision aligns with purpose, and every action sustains trust.

When practiced together, these five attributes transform leadership from authority into authenticity. They remind us that productive leadership is not about being in charge, but about *being of service* — turning clarity into care, and influence into impact.

CHAPTER 9
Levels of Productive Leadership
(John Maxwell Framework)

"Leadership is influence nothing more, nothing less."

— JOHN C. MAXWELL

No exploration of leadership would be complete without recognizing the enduring contribution of **John C. Maxwell**, whose *5 Levels of Leadership* transformed how millions understand influence.

His insight is timeless: leadership is not a title, but a **journey of influence**. Every level reflects a deeper relationship between who we are, what we do, and how we impact others.

In the context of the **Productive Leadership Model**, Maxwell's framework mirrors the same logic — leadership is not static; it evolves as self-awareness, character, and systems mature.

Each level represents a new depth of *trust, capability,* and *care*, all underpinned by the leader's mindset and moral compass.

PART 2 - FOCUS ON THE LEADER

The 5 Levels of Leadership

Leadership growth moves through five natural progressions of influence:

Position → Permission → Production → People Development → Pinnacle

These levels remind us that leadership influence is earned, not granted, and can differ from one relationship to another. A leader may be at Level 4 with one follower and still at Level 2 with another — because leadership is relational, not institutional.

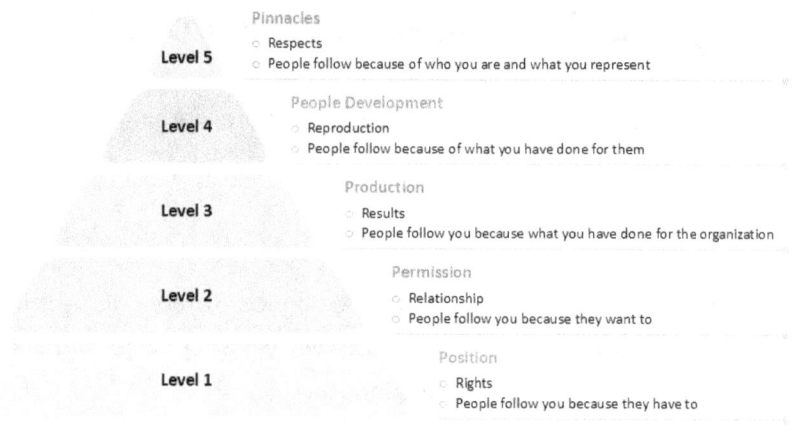

Figure 7: John Maxwell 5 Leadership Levels

What makes this model so powerful is that it mirrors real life. Leaders are not static. With one follower you may be at Level 2, while with another, depending on history, relationship, or trust you may still be at Level 1.

Level 1 – Position: People Follow Because They Have To

This is the entry point of leadership—authority by title, not trust. People follow because hierarchy says so.

While structure provides clarity, **positional power** alone is the weakest form of influence. It produces compliance, not commitment.

Examples:

- A new supervisor who relies on rules and policy rather than relationships.
- A military officer who holds rank but not respect.

Productive Leadership Link:
Position corresponds to the **Systems** block — establishing structure, process, and order. But systems without character and care will always fall short.

Guidance:
Use Level 1 to organize, but don't stay there. Ask yourself: *How am I earning followership beyond authority?*

Level 2 – Permission: People Follow Because They Want To

Here, leadership shifts from position to **relationship.** Influence flows from empathy, listening, and care. Trust replaces control.

People follow because they feel seen and respected.

Howard Schultz, founder of Starbucks, earned permission by valuing employees enough to offer healthcare to part-timers — a bold act of care that built loyalty.

Productive Leadership Link:
Permission connects to **Purpose and Values.** When leaders act with authenticity and respect, they activate emotional engagement.

Guidance:
Invest in relationships and empathy. Ask: *Do my people follow me because they trust me or because they must follow me?*

Level 3 – Production: People Follow Because of What You've Done for the Organization

At Level 3, influence is built on **results.** People follow because they see impact. It's leadership through competence and credibility.

Lee Kuan Yew transformed Singapore from a struggling island to a global powerhouse — proof that consistent results amplify influence.

Productive Leadership Link:
Production aligns with **Focus and Results** in the Productive Leadership Framework. It's where strategic clarity meets disciplined execution.

Guidance:
Deliver measurable outcomes that create shared wins. Ask: *Do my results elevate only me — or do they advance us all?*

Level 4 – People Development: People Follow Because of What You've Done for Them

True leadership multiplies itself. At Level 4, leaders shift from producing results to **producing other leaders.**

They empower, mentor, and delegate authority so others can succeed independently. **Jack Welch** at GE and **Bill Campbell**, "The Trillion-Dollar Coach," exemplified this—they built legacies by building others.

Productive Leadership Link:
This level expresses **Care and Courage**—the courage to release control and the care to invest in people's growth. It turns leadership from transaction into transformation.

Guidance:
Mentor intentionally. Share credit generously. Ask: *Who am I developing to lead when I'm gone?*

Level 5 – Pinnacle: People Follow Because of Who You Are and What You Represent

This is the summit—leadership grounded in **character and legacy.** At this level, influence transcends results; it becomes moral authority.

People follow you not because of what you have achieved, but because of *who you are.*

Nelson Mandela embodied Level 5. After 27 years in prison, he led South Africa with forgiveness rather than vengeance. His integrity inspired unity and global respect.

KEYS TO PRODUCTIVE LEADERSHIP

Productive Leadership Link:
Pinnacle corresponds with **Energy and Magnetism** in the Framework—the aura of authenticity that inspires voluntary followership.

Guidance:
You cannot chase the Pinnacle; you become it. Ask: Does my leadership still depend on title—or on trust?

Linking Levels to Sources of Power

Each level of leadership draws from different power dynamics:

Level	Why People Follow	Primary Source of Power
Level 1 – Position	Role or authority	Legitimate Power
Level 2 – Permission	Relationship & trust	Referent Power
Level 3 – Production	Proven results & competence	Expert + Reward Power
Level 4 – People Development	Growth of others	Expert (mentorship) + Referent Power
Level 5 – Pinnacle	Character & legacy	Moral Authority & Values

Recognizing these connections helps leaders understand *why* people follow them today and *how* they can expand influence tomorrow.

In the **Productive Leadership Model**, movement through these levels represents the evolution from **managing systems** → **leading people** → **building legacies.**

Case Study 4
Nelson Mandela: A Pinnacle Leader

Few leaders embody the upper levels as powerfully as Nelson Mandela. Imprisoned 27 years under apartheid, he emerged not with anger but with purpose — to heal his nation.

- **Level 1 (Position):** Mandela gained authority as President of South Africa in 1994, yet never relied solely on his office.
- **Level 2 (Permission):** His humility and empathy won hearts; even his jailers respected him.
- **Level 3 (Production):** He delivered measurable transformation — ending apartheid, establishing democracy, stabilizing a divided country.
- **Level 4 (People Development):** He nurtured new leaders and stepped aside after one term — an act of trust and foresight.
- **Level 5 (Pinnacle):** His influence endures through moral authority — a symbol of forgiveness and justice that outlives his presidency.

Mandela's life proves the highest level of leadership cannot be granted — it must be earned through purpose, patience, and principle.

Exercise 7: Mapping Your Leadership Levels

Choose three people you lead today. For each, reflect on the following:

1. At which level of leadership am I with this person today?

_____

_____

2. What source of power is my influence based on—position, relationship, results, development, or legacy?

_____

_____

3. What specific action can I take this month to move up one level with them?

_____

_____

See the Leadership Style Self-Assessment in Part 5 for a guided evaluation of your influence and growth path.

The journey through the *Levels of Productive Leadership* is the story of how leaders evolve from **authority to authenticity.** Position builds structure. Permission builds trust. Production builds results. People Development builds legacy. Pinnacle builds history.

Each step demands growth — in mindset, empathy, systems, and courage. The ultimate test is not whether people follow because they must, but whether they continue to follow when they no longer have to.

That is the mark of *productive leadership by influence.*

CHAPTER 10

The Productive Leader

"You do not rise to the level of your goals. You fall to the level of your systems." —

JAMES CLEAR

The Measure of Leadership

Every act of leadership eventually confronts one uncompromising question: **did it create value or did it cause harm?** History remembers both kinds of leaders.

Adolf Hitler mobilized millions, rebuilt industry, and revived a collapsing economy—yet his outcomes were poisoned by hate. The roads he paved led to ruin.

Sir Alex Ferguson, by contrast, spent twenty-seven years building not only one of the most successful football clubs in history but a living system of excellence, discipline, and growth. Both men achieved results; only one produced results that improved lives.

The difference lies not in effort but in *intent*. Results without conscience are destruction disguised as achievement. Results guided by purpose, systems, and care become legacy. The *productive leader* therefore measures success not by the noise of applause but by the quiet endurance of impact.

Beyond Performance

In the **Productive Leadership Model**, results are not the finish line—they are the mirror that reflects whether purpose, systems, and behaviour are aligned. Yet not all results are equal. Some are loud and short-lived, others quiet and eternal.

Performance results are driven by metrics—speed, profit, volume. They reward momentum but depend on constant pressure. Productive results, however, are measured by impact—by people who thrive, cultures that persist, and institutions that continue to grow long after the leader has left. One ends with exhaustion; the other with expansion.

Leaders are often celebrated for *what* they achieve, but history redeems only those who cared *how* they achieved it.

The Anatomy of Productive Results

Every sustainable achievement rests on three foundations.

First, **Purpose.** It is the moral compass that gives meaning to motion. Goals without purpose may create movement, but seldom progress. Purpose transforms ambition into contribution; it ensures that what we build serves more than our own reflection.

Second, **Systems.** They are the architecture that turns excellence into habit. Great leaders design structures that make good decisions repeatable and performance predictable. Systems outlast inspiration; they preserve wisdom when enthusiasm fades.

Third, **Humanity.** Results are not truly positive unless they elevate people. When success depletes the very energy that created it, it becomes self-destructive. The productive leader protects the human spirit as carefully as the balance sheet.

"The measure of a man is what he does with power." — Plato

Power in the hands of a productive leader is not an instrument of control but a means of creation—a force that multiplies potential rather than monopolising it.

The Cost of Negative Results

When ambition outruns ethics, achievement becomes toxic. Leaders who prize speed over substance or ego over empathy may deliver impressive numbers, but they leave behind hollow systems and disillusioned people. Negative results look successful until you measure their aftermath: fatigue, fear, and fragmentation.

If a victory drains more life than it gives, it is not a victory. The productive leader understands that results which require casualties are not achievements—they are warnings. Great leadership never asks people to trade their dignity for the leader's dream.

Case Study 5
Sir Alex Ferguson—Building a Legacy of Productive Results

Sir Alex Ferguson's career at Manchester United is a study in how purpose, systems, and humanity converge into enduring success. When he arrived in 1986, the club was fractured and uncertain. By the time he retired in 2013, it had become a global symbol of consistency and character.

Ferguson began with a clear purpose: to restore United to greatness through discipline, teamwork, and relentless self-belief. From that purpose he built systems—scouting networks, youth academies, and performance routines—that ensured success was structural, not accidental. He invested deeply in people, trusting young players and turning them into legends. Beckham, Giggs, Scholes, Ronaldo—each began as promise; under his guidance, each became proof.

What distinguished Ferguson was not the number of trophies—thirty-eight major titles, including thirteen Premier Leagues and two Champions Leagues—but the resilience of the culture he created. His mantra was simple: *no one is bigger than the club*. He demanded excellence, accepted mistakes, and renewed his teams generation after generation. His genius lay in continuity: adapting without abandoning values.

When Ferguson stepped down, he left behind more than victories; he left behind a living organism of excellence. His leadership demonstrated that When purpose and systems align with respect for people, results become regenerative. That is the essence of *productive leadership*.

From Results to Responsibility

Results are not rewards; they are responsibilities. They testify to whether our influence heals or harms, whether our systems strengthen or suffocate. The productive leader treats every outcome as feedback: a mirror reflecting the integrity of the process that produced it.

Instead of asking, *"What did I gain?"* *productive* leaders ask,

"What did we build that will last?"

"Who became stronger because I led?"

"Will this system still serve when I am gone?"

Those questions transform leadership from performance into stewardship. They shift the narrative from achievement to accountability—from success as ownership to success as obligation.

Exercise 8: The Results Mirror

Take a moment to examine your own outcomes.

1. What have you built this year that will endure?

_____

_____

2. Which successes elevated others, and which merely exhausted them?

_____

_____

3. What habits or systems ensure that progress continues in your absence?

_____

_____

True productivity is continuity without presence—the moment your influence sustains itself through others. The reflection may be confronting, but it is the birthplace of maturity. Leadership, after all, is not proven when we are in control, but when we are no longer required to be.

The productive leader is not driven by recognition but by regeneration—the quiet satisfaction of seeing systems thrive, people flourish, and values persist. They understand that the greatest result is not applause but advancement, not fame but flourishing.

When purpose shapes ambition and systems protect humanity, leadership transcends performance and becomes principle. That is the moment leadership turns from achievement into legacy.

"Try not to become a person of success, but rather try to become a person of value."
— *Albert Einstein*

The final measure of leadership is not the magnitude of its results but the morality of their impact. *Productive results* endure because they are built on purpose, strengthened by systems, and expressed through people. When success can stand alone—ethical, human, and sustainable—the leader has accomplished the rarest of feats: they have turned performance into permanence.

PART 2 - FOCUS ON THE LEADER

Part II: Summary

Leadership begins within. Before anyone can mobilize others, they must master the person they bring into every situation. Part II explores that inner journey — the disciplines, beliefs, and frameworks that turn a leader's intention into productive impact.

It opens with **self-awareness**: leadership starts not with position but with *mindset* — the ability to regulate thoughts, emotions, and choices. From this awareness flows **influence**, expressed through adaptive modes that match each situation and follower. Productive leaders do not cling to a single style; they read context and respond with precision and care.

Next comes **structure**. *The Productive Leader's Framework* reveals leadership as architecture — a system built on ten interconnected blocks: purpose, power, values, vision, focus, systems, traits and behaviors, results, personality and intelligence, and energy and magnetism. These form the bridge between who the leader is and what the leader builds.

Character then takes center stage through the **5 Cs of Productive Leadership — Character, Competence, Communication, Courage, and Care.** Together they shape trust, credibility, clarity, conviction, and compassion — the moral texture of productive leadership.

Growth continues through the **Levels of Leadership**, where influence matures from authority (Position) to relationship (Permission), to results (Production), to people development (Level 4), and finally to legacy (Pinnacle). This model mirrors the evolution from control to creation — from managing systems to building successors.

Part II concludes with **The Productive Leader**, a meditation on *results with conscience*. It distinguishes performance from productivity: the former achieves numbers; the latter sustains meaning. Leaders are judged not by how much they deliver but by how ethically, systemically, and humanely they do so. Positive results — those that elevate people and endure beyond the leader — are the ultimate proof of mastery.

In the Productive Leadership Model, the Leader is both architect and anchor — shaping mindset, structure, and spirit. Part II reveals that leadership excellence is neither an accident nor a gift; it is the deliberate alignment of **purpose, systems, and people** toward outcomes that create value without harm.

When leaders lead themselves with clarity, influence others with care, and design systems that endure, they transcend performance and enter the realm of legacy.

This is the essence of the **Productive Leader** — the one who turns vision into structure, structure into culture, and culture into results that last.

PART 3
FOCUS ON THE FOLLOWERS

Part III: Introduction

> *"A leader without followers is just taking a walk."*
>
> JOHN C. MAXWELL

Leadership is only half the equation. The other half—often forgotten, rarely studied—is followership. No leader, however gifted, can be productive in isolation. Productivity is not born from authority alone; it emerges from the dynamic partnership between the leader's intention and the follower's engagement.

In traditional leadership literature, followers are treated as the background—the supporting cast in the leader's story. Yet, in the **Productive Leadership Model**, followers are the co-authors of success. They are not commanded into contribution; they are inspired into commitment. Their trust gives leadership legitimacy, their energy gives it motion, and their growth gives it meaning.

A **productive follower** is not defined by obedience, but by ownership. They think, decide, and act in alignment with shared purpose. They hold the leader accountable, provide honest feedback, and protect the culture from complacency. They are courageous enough to dissent when silence would harm, and loyal enough to serve even when unseen.

This part explores the anatomy of that partnership — how leaders cultivate environments where followers don't just comply but contribute. It examines the psychology, behavior, and systems that transform passive participation into active co-creation. Through this lens, followership becomes not a lesser act but a leadership role in its own right.

Chapter 11 defines followership as a discipline — a conscious practice of trust, accountability, and initiative.

Chapter 12 explores the types of followers, from passive to proactive, showing how each shapes team performance.

Chapter 13 investigates the psychology of engagement — what makes people choose to give their best, and how leaders either ignite or inhibit that choice.

Chapter 14 introduces the concept of Partnership Power — the shared space where leader and follower meet as equals in purpose, united by respect and responsibility.

Together, these chapters form the bridge between influence and impact. They remind us that leadership is not a solo act but a social contract — one sustained by trust, communication, and mutual accountability.

In the **Productive Leadership Model**, the true measure of leadership is not how many follows, but how many grow because they did.

Leadership achieves permanence only when it elevates others to lead alongside it.

CHAPTER 11

The Productive Follower

"One of the greatest gifts a leader can give is the space for others to lead."

— SIMON SINEK

The Forgotten Half of Leadership

Leadership does not exist without followership. Every productive leader stands on the shoulders of followers who think, act, and decide with ownership. Yet in much of leadership literature, followers are treated as secondary — executors of the leader's vision, not co-creators of it.

In the **Productive Leadership Model**, followership is not a supporting role; it is *the other half of productivity*. A productive follower is not defined by obedience but by responsibility. They think critically, act purposefully, and hold themselves accountable for results as much as their leaders do. They do not wait for direction — they *anticipate*, they *contribute*, and they *care*.

While leaders set the tone, followers generate the tempo. They convert leadership's intent into operational excellence. They close the gap between vision and execution, transforming purpose into performance. Productive followership, therefore, is leadership practiced from the second chair.

PART 3 - FOCUS ON THE FOLLOWERS

1. The Mindset of the Productive Follower

Productive followers begin with mindset. They understand that influence is not owned by titles; it flows through initiative, integrity, and contribution.

Their mindset is rooted in **three disciplines**:

- **Self-Accountability:** They do not wait to be managed. They manage themselves. They take ownership of outcomes, deadlines, and learning.
- **Curiosity:** They ask *why* before they act. They seek to understand purpose, not just process.
- **Growth:** They see followership as a preparation for leadership. Every challenge becomes a classroom for developing competence and confidence.

In essence, productive followers see themselves as *partners in purpose*. They don't simply support leaders — they strengthen them.

2. The Behaviors of the Productive Follower

Mindset alone is not enough. Productive followers express their commitment through consistent behaviors that strengthen the system:

- **Communication:** They speak truth to power — respectfully but clearly. They surface issues before they escalate, ensuring decisions are informed, not impulsive.
- **Initiative:** They don't wait for instructions to act. They anticipate needs, solve problems, and improve processes without being told.
- **Constructive Dissent:** They challenge ideas, not people. Productive followers understand that disagreement, when expressed with respect, protects the organization from blind spots.
- **Reliability:** Their word is their bond. Leaders learn they can depend on them, not just for output, but for judgment.
- **Collaboration:** They share credit, build trust, and elevate others. They recognize that leadership is not competition; it is coordination.

Through these behaviors, productive followers turn alignment into engagement and engagement into momentum.

3. The Partnership Between Leader and Follower

In a productive system, leadership and followership form a **reciprocal loop**. Each depends on the other for clarity, trust, and progress.

- The **leader** provides vision, context, and trust.
- The **follower** provides feedback, discipline, and execution.

When both operate within shared purpose and transparent systems, their relationship becomes partnership — a cycle of mutual accountability. This is where the *Productive Leadership Model* reaches its full maturity: leadership is not a hierarchy, but a network of shared responsibility.

Followers who think like owners expand the leader's capacity. Leaders who empower such followers multiply impact. This is the essence of **productive partnership**.

Case Study 6
NASA Mission Control – The Power of Empowered Followers

In April 1970, NASA's Apollo 13 mission was crippled by an explosion that disabled the spacecraft's oxygen and power systems, leaving three astronauts stranded nearly 200,000 miles from Earth. The world remembers the phrase, "Houston, we've had a problem."

What followed was one of the greatest displays of *productive followership* in human history. Inside NASA's Mission Control, a team of engineers, scientists, and technicians — none with ultimate command authority — took ownership of solving an impossible problem.

They were followers, not commanders, yet they led from within.

Working under immense pressure, these teams demonstrated every dimension of the productive follower mindset:

- **Purpose Alignment:** Their goal was singular and clear — bring the astronauts home alive. Every decision was filtered through that purpose.
- **Systems Thinking:** They used discipline and procedure to guide creativity. Every test, simulation, and calculation was documented and verified through a system, not guesswork.
- **Courageous Dissent:** Engineers challenged assumptions fearlessly. When one system failed, another spoke up with alternatives. There was no fear of hierarchy — only focus on results.
- **Collaboration:** Mission Control worked as a living organism. Each console represented expertise; together they became collective intelligence.

As Gene Kranz, the Flight Director, later wrote:

"There was no time for blame. There was only time for solutions."

Apollo 13 was safely brought home because followers acted like leaders — thinking critically, working cohesively, and staying faithful to the mission's purpose. Their success remains a timeless lesson: *when leadership is distributed, productivity becomes unstoppable.*

Exercise 9: The Mirror of Followership

Take a moment to reflect on your current role and team.

1. How do you demonstrate ownership without authority?

_____

_____

2. When was the last time you spoke up to protect a shared purpose?

_____

_____

3. What behaviors make you a partner rather than a participant?

_____

_____

4. How can you develop others around you to lead from where they stand?

_____

_____

Leadership grows when followership matures. The best followers elevate everyone — including their leaders.

In the *Productive Leadership Model*, leadership is not defined by direction but by **connection**. Productive followers turn the leader's intent into collective momentum. They embody accountability without authority and courage without recognition.

The most productive teams are not those with the strongest leader, but those with the *strongest followers*.

"A leader is only as strong as the people who believe enough to follow."

— Ali Kasa

CHAPTER 12

The Leader, Follower Model

"I am not afraid of an army of lions led by a sheep; I am afraid of an army of sheep led by a lion."

— ALEXANDER THE GREAT

Leadership as Partnership

Leadership is never a solo act. It is a partnership — an ongoing exchange between leaders and followers, sustained by trust and animated by purpose. Leaders bring direction and vision; followers bring energy and execution. Together they orbit around something far greater than either of them alone: the shared *why* that gives their work meaning.

In the **Productive Leadership Model**, leadership and followership exist in a continuous cycle of mutual reinforcement. When purpose is clear, leaders and followers strengthen each other. When it fades, the system fractures — leadership collapses into authority without inspiration, and followership decays into compliance without commitment.

Productive leadership, therefore, is not defined by hierarchy but by **alignment** — the synchronization of influence and response around a shared purpose

PART 3 - FOCUS ON THE FOLLOWERS

The Leader–Follower Loop

At the heart of the Leader–Follower Model lies a living loop — a cycle that governs all productive organizations:

1. **Leaders influence followers** through their vision, values, and example.
2. **Followers respond** through trust, courage, and contribution.
3. **Purpose binds** both, creating gravitational alignment.

This loop is not linear; it is circular and regenerative. Leaders influence followers. Followers' response shapes the leader's credibility. Purpose acts as gravity, holding both in orbit.

When purpose is strong, the loop accelerates: leaders inspire → followers engage → results build trust → trust amplifies influence. When purpose weakens, the loop decays — frustration rises, blame circulates, and the system loses energy.

Leadership and followership thrive only when they revolve around the same sun — the purpose that lights their shared path. The diagram below illustrated how leaders and follower revolve around purpose.

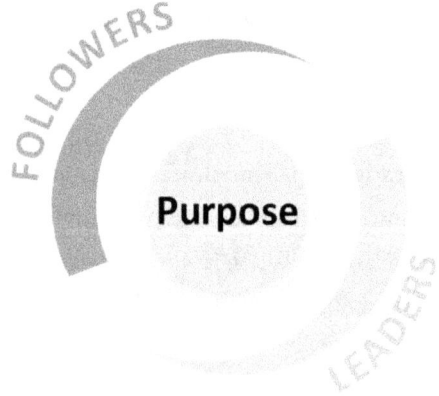

Figure 8: Leader–Follower Loop

Why Purpose Matters

As Simon Sinek teaches, *people don't buy what you do; they buy why you do it.* Purpose is leadership's gravitational force. It pulls energy into focus, keeps direction steady, and transforms motion into meaning.

- **For leaders**, purpose provides clarity — it guards against ego and distraction.
- **For followers**, purpose provides meaning — it converts effort into contribution.
- **For organizations**, purpose provides alignment — it harmonizes leader and follower energy around something greater than personal interest.

Purpose is not a slogan. It is the invisible architecture of performance. Without it, leaders rely on control and followers resort to compliance. With it, influence becomes self-sustaining — loyalty, innovation, and trust all orbit naturally around the collective *why*.

History has proved this truth again and again:

- **Gandhi's followers** endured hardship because they believed in the purpose of nonviolent freedom.
- **NASA's engineers** worked tirelessly not to "assemble rockets," but to *put a man on the moon and bring him safely home.*

Purpose transforms ordinary effort into extraordinary endurance.

Personal Story

On one consulting assignment, I inherited a project team that included three employees on the verge of being fired. Leadership had already deemed them "useless." They were demotivated, detached, and seen as liabilities.

Instead of accepting that verdict, I met with each of them individually. I listened to their stories, skills, and frustrations. What I found surprised me: they weren't useless they were unaligned. They lacked clarity of purpose.

I brought them into my project, gave them responsibilities tied directly to a meaningful outcome, and connected their work to the bigger picture. The transformation was dramatic. They went from disengaged to energized, delivering outstanding results. By the end of the project, all three had been promoted to departmental leadership roles.

That experience taught me a vital truth: there are no useless followers only misaligned purposes. When followers connect to why their work matters, potential that seemed invisible suddenly becomes undeniable.

Shared Purpose as the Gravitational Center

Shared purpose is the invisible force that binds leaders and followers in a productive orbit. It is the reason they keep showing up, the fuel that sustains them when pressure mounts.

- Without shared purpose, the loop becomes fragile. Commands are issued, tasks are completed, but the bond is mechanical. Performance may occur, but loyalty and sustainability do not.
- With shared purpose, leadership and followership reinforce each other. The leader inspires; the follower commits. Trust deepens, initiative expands, and results endure.

Purpose is gravity — unseen but unyielding. It keeps people aligned when uncertainty shakes the system. It gives both leader and follower the reason to persevere, even when results are not immediate.

Exercise 10: Aligning Around Shared Purpose

1. What is the purpose that connects me and my team beyond daily tasks?

_____

_____

_____

2. Do my followers understand this purpose in a way that excites them?

___

3. How can I reshape roles and responsibilities so that every follower sees how their work contributes to something larger?

___

The Leader–Follower Model reminds us: leadership is not a one-way act of direction, but a two-way flow of energy. It is a loop of influence and response, held together by shared purpose. Leaders set direction, followers respond, but purpose keeps both aligned. When purpose is missing, followers drift and leaders blame. But when purpose is strong, even the weakest followers can rise, and even the boldest leader can sustain influence.

As Alexander the Great observed, an army of sheep led by a lion is far more powerful than an army of lions led by a sheep. The quality of leadership magnifies the quality of followership but only when both revolve around a purpose greater than themselves.

CHAPTER 13

The Courageous Followers Model

"The ultimate measure of a person is not where they stand in moments of comfort and convenience, but where they stand in times of challenge and controversy."

— MARTIN LUTHER KING JR.

The Courage to Follow

Most leadership writing celebrates the courage of those who stand in front—the leaders who take risks, make decisions, and confront uncertainty. Yet leadership is only half the story. For leadership to be truly productive, followers too must possess courage—the courage to commit, to speak truth, to embrace change, and, at times, to walk away.

Ira Chaleff's landmark work *The Courageous Follower* reframed followership as an active and responsible discipline. He argued that followers are not passive recipients of authority but partners who share accountability for outcomes. In the **Productive Leadership Model**, courageous followership is the stabilizing force that keeps the system ethical, balanced, and self-correcting. It prevents power from drifting into ego and keeps purpose at the center of gravity.

Chaleff identified **five dimensions of courageous followership**—five ways followers demonstrate strength, integrity, and partnership. Each reveals how courage sustains the productive loop between leaders and followers.

PART 3 - FOCUS ON THE FOLLOWERS

1. Courage to Assume Responsibility

Productive followers never wait for permission to add value. They recognize that responsibility is not granted by position but claimed through purpose. When they see what must be done, they step forward.

In every hospital ward there is a nurse who spots a risk and acts before a doctor gives orders; in every company there is a team member who notices a customer issue and resolves it instead of waiting. Such people understand that the shared purpose—the "why"—is everyone's to protect.

For leaders, this first dimension is an invitation to empower. Reward initiative, not blind obedience. Responsibility taken should be celebrated more than responsibility assigned.

2. Courage to Serve

Courage to serve is not servitude; it is devotion to purpose. It is the strength to bring one's best to a collective mission even when it demands sacrifice or discomfort.

History is filled with examples. Gandhi's followers endured imprisonment and violence not because they sought glory, but because they believed deeply in the cause of independence. Their courage was not expressed in speeches, but in endurance.

In modern organizations, this courage appears when individuals give extra effort not out of fear, but out of pride in excellence and loyalty to values. Leaders who connect tasks to meaning ignite this type of courage; followers who see how their work matters sustain it

3. Courage to Challenge

The third dimension is the most demanding. It is the moral resolve to confront what is wrong, even when the source of that wrong is authority itself. Courageous followers protect the shared purpose when silence would betray it.

Abraham Lincoln surrounded himself with a *team of rivals*—strong-minded advisors who argued, questioned, and sharpened his decisions. Their disagreements strengthened the nation. By contrast, when challenge is absent, disaster follows.

In the 1980s, **Korean Air** suffered a series of fatal crashes. Investigators discovered that co-pilots had often recognized the captain's errors but failed to speak up—silenced by hierarchy and fear. The absence of courageous followership proved deadly. Only after the airline rebuilt its culture, empowering junior officers to challenge senior pilots, did its safety record transform. The lesson is timeless: without the courage to challenge, expertise and talent remain powerless.

Leaders who value truth over comfort create space for this courage to thrive. They understand that respectful dissent is not rebellion—it is responsibility

4. Courage to Participate in Transformation

Change unsettles people. It disrupts systems, habits, and identities. Yet productive organizations depend on followers who participate actively in transformation rather than resist it.

When Satya Nadella took over Microsoft, he replaced a culture of rivalry with one of learning. His vision of a *growth mindset* demanded followers brave enough to question old habits, learn new skills, and rebuild processes. Their courage turned an aging corporation into a rejuvenated innovator.

For followers, this dimension means leaning into discomfort as part of progress. For leaders, it means explaining *why* transformation matters and equipping people to succeed in the new reality. When both commit, change becomes renewal instead of rupture.

5. Courage to Leave

Sometimes the highest expression of courage is departure. When a culture becomes toxic or a purpose unethical, followers may serve integrity best by walking away. This decision is never easy—it costs security, belonging, even identity—but it preserves moral clarity.

History honors those who resigned rather than compromise ethics. In business, in government, in faith institutions, such departures have often sparked reform. Leaving is not betrayal; it is loyalty to a deeper principle.

Leaders who respect such decisions demonstrate maturity. They recognize that the courage to leave is a mirror reflecting where the culture has drifted from its values.

Personal Story

In one of my assignments, I met a group of project managers frustrated by delays, billing issues, and quality concerns. Tension filled the room until one manager said sharply, "We report to our CEOs, not to you."

I paused, then asked them: "In an operating theatre, the nurse goes through a checklist with the doctor. Who reports to whom?" They answered: "The nurse reports to the doctor."

"Correct," I said. "But why does the nurse go through the checklist? Because both share the same purpose: to save the patient."

That reframed the conversation. It wasn't about reporting lines. It was about courage to assume responsibility, to serve, and sometimes to challenge. Just as Korean Air's disasters showed the cost of silence, productive organizations depend on followers who speak up for the shared purpose.

Exercise 11: Cultivating Courageous Followership

1. Which of the five dimensions of courage do I see most in my team?

_____

_____

_____

2. Which dimension do I need to model as a leader to encourage in my followers?

_____

_____

_____

3. What practical step can I take this quarter to create a culture where courage is expected, not feared?

_____

_____

_____

Courageous followership is not rebellion—it is responsibility in motion. It is the conscience of productive leadership: the voice that speaks when silence would endanger purpose, the hand that helps when others hesitate, the heart that stays true when convenience tempts compromise.

Leaders who surround themselves with courageous followers rise higher. Followers who act with courage make leaders better. And organizations that cultivate courage on both sides build resilience, integrity, and results that endure.

CHAPTER 14
The Productive Follower Growth System

> *"The function of leadership is to produce more leaders, not more followers."*
>
> — RALPH NADER

Leaders Who Build Leaders

The measure of leadership lies not only in results but in the quality of people it cultivates. Productive leaders don't seek followers who depend on them; they build followers who can think, decide, and lead independently.

Followers rarely grow by accident. They grow by design — through systems, cultures, and habits that transform compliance into courage and repetition into reflection.

The **Productive Follower Growth System** provides the architecture for that design: six interlinked tools that guide followers from dependency toward self-leadership.

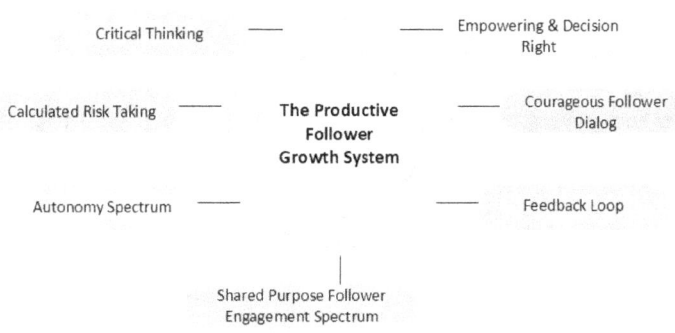

Figure 9: The Productive Follower Growth System

PART 3 - FOCUS ON THE FOLLOWERS

Tool 1: The Follower Engagement Spectrum

Every organization houses a spectrum of followership.

At one end are the *passive* — disengaged and doing the minimum. In the middle are the *compliant* — cooperative but cautious. At the far end are the *courageous partners* — proactive, creative, and committed to shared purpose.

The leader's task is to move followers along this spectrum through awareness and connection.

A manufacturing firm once discovered that 60 percent of its employees viewed themselves as merely compliant. Instead of reprimand, leaders initiated purpose workshops and recognition programs. Within months, engagement scores and productivity rose.

Leaders who revisit this spectrum regularly create a rhythm of reflection: *Where is each person today, and what will help them move one step closer to partnership?*

Tool 2: Shared Purpose Alignment

Followers flourish when they understand *why* their work matters. Shared purpose turns routine effort into meaningful contribution.

Ask together:

1. Why do we exist?
2. Who do we serve?
3. How does my role contribute?

In the 1960s, when a NASA janitor said, "I'm helping put a man on the moon," he revealed the power of purpose alignment — identity woven into mission.

Purpose is leadership's gravity. Without it, followers drift. With it, they unite around something greater than personal ambition.

Tool 3: Courageous Follower Dialogue

Courageous followers speak truth with respect. They challenge decisions that threaten the shared purpose. Productive leaders welcome this challenge, knowing that silence is far riskier than dissent.

When a global bank adopted the *Courageous Follower Checklist*, employees admitted they felt free to serve but not to challenge. The leaders responded by holding *safe-voice sessions* where people could raise concerns without penalty. Trust — and performance — surged.

Challenge is not rebellion; it is responsibility voiced with respect.

Tool 4: Feedback Loops That Build Trust

Feedback is the oxygen of growth, yet in many organizations it flows only downward.

Productive leaders create **two-way feedback loops** where information and insight travel freely.

After Google's *Project Oxygen* study, managers who practiced upward feedback improved most. Asking *"What could I have done differently to help you succeed?"* became a ritual of humility.

Simple conversations — *Start, Stop, Continue* — transform teams. Over time, feedback becomes a shared language of progress, not a system of judgment.

Tool 5: Delegation, Empowerment & Decision Rights

Empowerment without clarity breeds chaos; clarity without empowerment breeds dependency. The balance is achieved through **structured delegation**.

In productive cultures, leaders delegate not just tasks but trust. They clarify who **Decides**, who **Contributes**, and who must be **Informed**. This Decision-Rights framework transforms authority into accountability.

At Ritz-Carlton, every employee may spend up to $2,000 to solve a guest problem instantly. The amount is symbolic — it tells employees, *We trust your judgment.*

PART 3 - FOCUS ON THE FOLLOWERS

Delegation is not abdication. It is the deliberate transfer of power that multiplies ownership. When followers act with authority, they grow into leaders.

Tool 6: The Autonomy Spectrum Model

Not all followers are ready for complete independence — and that's natural. Leadership means calibrating freedom to readiness.

The **Autonomy Spectrum Model** shows this progression, ranging from *Directive* to *Autonomous*.

Leaders adjust style as competence and confidence rise — replacing control with trust step by step.

Figure 10: The Autonomy Spectrum

Aviation illustrates this perfectly: a new co-pilot follows strict checklists, while an experienced captain exercises discretion. The same principle applies in business, art, and science. The leader's goal is not control but calibration — guiding followers until they can guide themselves.

The Culture of Calculated Risk

Empowerment has no value without permission to make mistakes.

A culture that punishes every error kills initiative; a culture that learns from errors breeds innovation.

Productive leaders normalize *learning through risk*. They review what went wrong without blame and celebrate the insight gained. Mistakes become data, not disgrace.

In such an environment, followers take ownership, test ideas, and grow resilience — the hallmark of a thriving system.

The Discipline of Critical Thinking

In the age of instant information, many have outsourced thought to algorithms. Convenience has replaced contemplation.

But no machine can replace discernment — the human ability to question assumptions, weigh consequences, and act ethically.

Productive leaders teach their followers to think, not just to know. They foster curiosity, dialogue, and debate. They ask *"What evidence supports this?"*, *"What could we be missing?"* and *"What are the unintended consequences?"*

Critical thinking is not rebellion; it is responsibility in an era of noise. It ensures that leadership remains human even as technology accelerates.

Personal Story

In my current role, I made a commitment to invest deeply in my team's growth. Each member has an **individual development plan** that we co-create. They articulate their growth objectives, and I ensure they have the tools to pursue them.

Every team member has a **LinkedIn Premium account** to access LinkedIn Learning. Together, we agree on a list of books, and I send weekly learning suggestions. I track both the **time and cash investment** each person makes monthly in their development because I want them to see that the best investment they can make is in themselves.

But development is not just personal it is collective. Each team member is required to do **knowledge sharing with juniors**, teaching what they learn to others. This multiplies growth across the team.

I've seen remarkable results. People who once doubted their potential are now stepping into bigger roles with confidence. The tools are important, but even more important is the message: I believe in you enough to invest in your growth.

Exercise 12: Designing My Follower Growth System

1. Which element of the Productive Follower Growth System will most accelerate my team's growth right now?

_____

_____

2. How can I introduce it without overwhelming the team's rhythm?

_____

_____

3. What signals will tell me that followers are evolving into leaders?

_____

_____

Followers don't grow by chance; they grow by design.

They flourish in environments where courage is safe, purpose is clear, and mistakes are treated as lessons. They thrive when trusted to decide, encouraged to think, and allowed to learn through risk.

A productive leader's greatest legacy is not how many followers they command, but how many leaders they leave behind—individuals capable of sustaining purpose long after the original voice has stepped aside.

Part 3: Summary

Leadership is not a solo act — it is a shared performance between those who lead and those who choose to follow. This part repositions followers from passive recipients to *active partners* in the leadership process. The productivity of leadership depends as much on the quality of followership as on the character of the leader.

From Obedience to Partnership

The part opens with the recognition that followers give leadership its energy, accountability, and direction. Chapter 11 redefines followership as the *forgotten half of leadership*, illustrating through the NASA case how engaged, responsible followers amplify vision, safeguard integrity, and ensure excellence. Productive followership is not submission but *shared stewardship* of purpose.

The Leader-Follower Dynamic

Chapter 12 explores the **Leader–Follower Loop**, a continuous cycle of influence and feedback. It shows that leadership becomes productive when followers are engaged, informed, and aligned with purpose. This loop transforms hierarchy into partnership and dependency into dialogue. The leader sets direction; followers reflect and refine it — together creating alignment around shared meaning.

Courage as the Catalyst

Chapter 13 introduces Ira Chaleff's **Courageous Follower Model**, reminding us that courage is not reserved for leaders alone. Followers demonstrate five types of courage — to assume responsibility, to serve, to challenge, to participate in transformation, and to leave when integrity demands it. Through the Korean Air case and personal reflections, the chapter emphasizes that silence is often more dangerous than dissent and that speaking up is a moral act of loyalty to purpose.

Growing Followers into Leaders

Chapter 14 presents **the Productive Follower Growth System**, integrating empowerment, critical thinking, and structured autonomy into a cohesive framework for follower development. It introduces practical tools — the Engagement Spectrum, Purpose Alignment Canvas, Courageous Follower Checklist, Feedback Loops, and Decision-Rights Matrix — culminating in the **Autonomy Spectrum Model**, where followers evolve from dependence to self-leadership.

The chapter underscores that leadership maturity is measured by how many leaders one creates, not how many followers one controls. Productive leaders build environments where mistakes are learning opportunities, risk-taking is encouraged, and curiosity replaces compliance. In the age of automation and AI, the hallmark of a great follower is *critical thinking* — the courage to question, reason, and improve the system.

The Essence of Productive Followership

Part 3 completes the second dimension of the **Productive Leadership Model** — the *Follower*. Where Part 2 focused on self-mastery, Part 3 extends that mastery into relationships of trust and collaboration. It shows that leadership thrives where followers are courageous, capable, and connected by shared purpose.

The productive organization is not a hierarchy but a *partnership network* — a community where everyone leads from where they stand. Leaders ignite, followers amplify, and together they sustain progress and purpose.

PART 4
FOCUS ON THE SITUATION

Part 4: Introduction

> *"The greatest danger in times of turbulence is not the turbulence; it is to act with yesterday's logic.".*
>
> PETER DRUCKER

Every act of leadership happens within a context — a specific set of conditions, constraints, and possibilities. No decision, no strategy, and no influence exists in a vacuum. The most brilliant leader and the most committed followers can still fail if they misread the environment they operate in.

That is why **situation** forms the *third pillar* of the **Productive Leadership Model**, completing the triad of **Leader → Follower → Situation**. If the *Leader* defines direction and the *Follower* provides energy, the *Situation* provides the terrain — the reality that tests every assumption and magnifies or limits impact.

Productive leaders master the art of **situational intelligence** — the ability to interpret reality clearly, adapt swiftly, and align people and systems to what the moment demands. They understand that leadership style is not a matter of preference but of relevance. What works in calm waters may fail in a storm.

This part explores how leaders read, navigate, and respond to different contexts — from complexity and uncertainty to crisis and transformation. You will learn how to:

- Adjust your leadership style to fit the readiness and capability of your followers.
- Lead effectively in volatile, uncertain, complex, and ambiguous (VUCA) environments.
- Communicate with authority and empathy during crises.
- Build systems and cultures that thrive through change, not just survive it.

The goal is not to make you a different kind of leader, but a *situationally aware* one — someone who sees the bigger picture, senses the undercurrents, and acts with clarity and composure.

As you move through the chapters that follow, think of yourself as a strategist and navigator — leading not only with intention but with interpretation. Because in leadership, as in life, it is not the strongest who endure, but those most adaptable to change.

CHAPTER 15

Leading Through Situational Awareness

"Constant change is the only thing certain in today's world."
— HERACLITUS

Leadership does not happen in isolation. Even the most talented leader with the most committed followers will falter if they misread the situation. **Context defines success.** Timing amplifies or destroys it. Circumstances can make or break even the best intentions.

In the **Productive Leadership Model**, *Situation* forms the third pillar of productive leadership — completing the triad of **Leader → Follower → Situation**. The leader defines direction, the follower provides energy, and the situation defines reality. The productive leader's strength lies not only in vision or influence but in the ability to *interpret* and *adapt* to that reality.

What works in one setting may fail in another. The style that inspires in a crisis may frustrate in calm periods. Followers who flourish under autonomy in one context may need closer direction in another. Leadership that ignores context quickly becomes irrelevant — or even destructive.

The Boiling Frog Analogy

There is an old metaphor: if you drop a frog into boiling water, it will jump out immediately. But if you place it in cool water and slowly raise the temperature, it will not notice the danger until it's too late.

PART 4 - FOCUS ON THE SITUATION

Many organizations behave the same way. They ignore gradual shifts in technology, culture, customer expectations, or regulation until the water around them boils. They wake up too late — overwhelmed by crises they could have prevented.

Understanding the situation means learning to sense the heat before it rises. **Productive leaders build systems of awareness** — listening deeply, scanning the environment, encouraging honest feedback, and responding before problems become irreversible.

Figure 11: Boiling Frog Analogy - Slow change kills faster than sudden shock.

Understanding the Lesson

The Boiling Frog Analogy reminds us that the greatest threat to leadership isn't sudden crisis — it's comfort. When leaders normalize small declines, tolerate mediocrity, or silence uncomfortable truths, they slowly drift toward irrelevance.

To avoid becoming the boiling frog, productive leaders:

- **Stay alert** — Monitor subtle environmental and cultural shifts.
- **Encourage inquiry** — Ask uncomfortable questions before problems grow.
- **Promote transparency** — Reward truth-telling and early reporting.
- **Act early** — Adjust course before the water gets hot.

Leader's Reflection:

Where might the "water" be warming around me?

_____

_____

_____

What subtle changes am I ignoring because they feel familiar?

_____

_____

_____

Personal Story

In my current role, I learned how easily leaders can misread situations by focusing only on symptoms. Each year, our group was paying significant penalties for non-compliance with local regulations. At first glance, it appeared to be a technical or procedural issue. But when I looked deeper, I realized it was cultural.

Our written values emphasized *accountability* and *ownership*, yet our policies punished mistakes by deducting fines from employees' salaries. The system unintentionally created fear, not responsibility. Employees hid errors rather than reported them.

We reframed accountability. Instead of punishment, we introduced transparent monthly violation reports and education sessions. We defined accountability not as *blame*, but as *ownership + learning*.

Within months, violations dropped, fines decreased, and — more importantly — conversation shifted from hiding problems to solving them. Teams began asking, "How do we prevent this next time?" rather than "How do I avoid blame?"

That experience taught me that **situational awareness begins with curiosity**. It is not only about scanning external risks but also about sensing cultural, emotional, and behavioral undercurrents. Until leaders diagnose what's really happening beneath the surface, no policy or directive can succeed.

Exercise 13: Spotting the Heat Before It Boils

1. Where might you be normalizing small warning signs — in performance, morale, or quality?

   _____

   _____

2. What shifts in your market, technology, or culture might be heating the water around you?

   _____

   _____

3. What early actions could prevent tomorrow's crisis?

   _____

   _____

Leadership without situational awareness is like sailing without navigation — you may be moving, but not necessarily in the right direction.

The productive leader sees reality clearly, acts early, and adapts continually. Because in a world of constant change, survival doesn't belong to the strongest or the smartest — but to those most aware of the temperature around them.

CHAPTER 16
Assessing Situations

"In preparing for battle, I have always found that plans are useless, but planning is indispensable."

— DWIGHT D. EISENHOWER

Leadership is not just about vision or charisma; it is about how accurately a leader reads reality. A brilliant plan executed in the wrong context will fail. A modest plan applied to the right situation may succeed. **Productive leaders** excel not because they know everything, but because they diagnose before they decide.

After developing awareness (the *why*), situational assessment becomes the *how* — the disciplined process of reading the environment, the organization, and the people before acting. It transforms intuition into intelligence.

Lessons from History: Misreading the Situation

Nokia was one of the earliest pioneers in smartphones. Long before the iPhone, they had touch-screen devices, advanced operating systems, and the technical capability to dominate the smartphone revolution. But they misread the situation in two ways.

First, they overestimated consumer readiness. When Nokia launched advanced phones, the mass market wasn't yet prepared for them. Second, when the market finally was ready, Nokia adopted a **flawed business model** building exclusive Nokia stores and refusing to partner with telecom operators. Phones remained expensive, limiting mass adoption.

Apple and Samsung, observing consumer behavior more accurately, did the opposite. They **partnered with operators**, subsidizing phones and making them affordable. They learned from Nokia's mistakes, adapted to the situation, and seized dominance. Nokia, despite its early lead, collapsed not because it lacked technology, but because it failed to read the situation.

Kodak is another cautionary tale. The company invented the digital camera in the 1970s but dismissed it, fearing it would cannibalize their highly profitable film business. Kodak saw the technology but failed to see the **consumer shift** that was coming: people no longer wanted to wait for photos they wanted instant results.

Competitors embraced digital photography, while Kodak clung to film. By the time they tried to pivot, it was too late. Kodak didn't fail because it lacked innovation. It failed because it assessed the situation narrowly through the lens of protecting old profits instead of anticipating new realities.

These cases remind us: **misreading the situation is more dangerous than lacking resources or ideas.** Leaders who assess situations wisely adapt and thrive; those who ignore or misdiagnose reality stumble, often fatally.

Why Assessment Matters

Every decision a leader makes rests on assumptions about the situation. If the assumptions are wrong, the decisions will be wrong. Leaders who act without assessing the situation are like doctors prescribing medicine without examining the patient. The symptoms may look familiar, but without diagnosis, the treatment may be harmful.

Situational assessment allows leaders to move from **reaction** to **preparation.** It turns vague impressions into structured understanding. It is not about eliminating uncertainty but about giving leaders the best possible reading of reality so they can adapt accordingly.

The Situational Assessment Framework

To assess situations productively, leaders can use a three-lens framework: external forces, internal conditions, and follower readiness.

External Forces

External forces define the landscape in which the organization operates market trends, competition, technology, regulations, and economic cycles. These forces change the rules of the game, often without warning.

Leaders must **scan broadly, test assumptions, and anticipate threats and opportunities.** Failure to do so leads to irrelevance. Nokia and Kodak show how ignoring external shifts destroys even the strongest companies. Netflix, in contrast, thrived because it read the external shift to streaming before others and pivoted early.

Key Reflection: What external changes regulatory, technological, competitive could reshape my industry tomorrow? Am I prepared?

Internal Conditions

If external forces are the waves, internal conditions are the strength of the boat. Culture, systems, processes, and morale determine whether an organization can ride the waves or sink beneath them.

A leader may see opportunity externally, but if internally the organization is siloed, fearful, or dysfunctional, the opportunity will be wasted. Satya Nadella's transformation of Microsoft is a textbook example. He saw that external competition was fierce, but he also recognized that the **real battle was internal.** By shifting culture from defensiveness to growth, collaboration, and openness, Microsoft became agile enough to compete again.

Key Reflection: Does my culture fuel or block execution? Do my systems and processes accelerate progress or slow it down? Is morale high enough to handle

Follower Readiness

Finally, even with clear external and internal analysis, leaders must ask: **Can my people deliver?** Follower readiness is often misunderstood as just competence and motivation. In reality, it rests on **four factors:**

1. **Competence:** Do they have the knowledge and skills?
2. **Commitment:** Do they have the willpower and energy to follow through?
3. **Trust:** Do I trust them to act responsibly, and do they trust me to lead fairly?
4. **Reliability:** Can I count on them to deliver consistently, not just occasionally?

PART 4 - FOCUS ON THE SITUATION

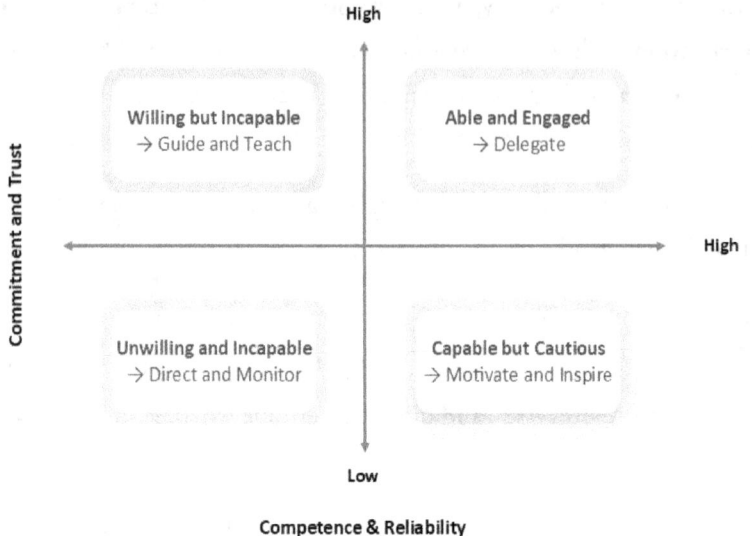

Figure 12: Follower Readiness Model

A follower who is competent but unreliable cannot be trusted with critical tasks. One who is reliable and competent but does not trust leadership will never fully engage. One who is motivated but lacks competence may have energy but deliver poor results. True readiness requires alignment across all four dimensions.

Key Reflection: With each follower, do I know their competence, commitment, trust level, and reliability? Am I leading them accordingly?

The Situational Assessment Matrix

Lens	Key Questions	Warning Signs	Leadership Response
External Forces	What trends or regulations affect us? What assumptions may change?	Ignoring competitors, dismissing new technologies	Scan environment, scenario plan, adapt early

KEYS TO PRODUCTIVE LEADERSHIP

Lens	Key Questions	Warning Signs	Leadership Response
Internal Conditions	What is our culture, morale, and system health?	Silos, fear, disengagement, weak processes	Strengthen culture, fix systems, build trust
Follower Readiness	Are my people competent, committed, trustworthy, and reliable?	High skills but low trust; high energy but low reliability	Adjust style: more direction, coaching, or empowerment depending on readiness

This matrix turns reflection into diagnosis. Leaders can use it before strategic decisions, during crises, or as part of quarterly reviews.

Exercise 14: My Situational Assessment

Choose one challenge your organization faces right now and ask:

1. **External Forces:** What outside pressures or opportunities shape this situation?

_____

_____

_____

2. **Internal Conditions:** What cultural, systemic, or morale issues affect us?

_____

_____

_____

PART 4 - FOCUS ON THE SITUATION

3. Follower Readiness: How would I rate my people on competence, commitment, trust, and reliability?

_____

_____

_____

4. Synthesis: What leadership adjustments does this situation demand from me?

_____

_____

_____

Situational assessment is a leader's radar. Without it, leaders fly blind — surprised by shocks, undermined by hidden weaknesses, or disappointed by misaligned teams. With it, they anticipate, adapt, and align their leadership to reality.

Productive leadership is never generic; it is situational. The best leaders don't just ask, *"What do I want to do?"* They ask, *"What does this situation demand of me — and how can I prepare my people to meet it?"*

CHAPTER 17

Matching Leadership Style with Situation

"The greatest danger in times of turbulence is not the turbulence; it is to act with yesterday's logic."

— PETER DRUCKER

Leadership is never static. The style that inspires in one situation may fail completely in another. **Productive leaders** adapt. They read the context, understand their followers' readiness, and adjust their behavior to serve the purpose best.

The most dangerous phrase in leadership is, *"This is just how I lead."*

Situational leadership demands humility to flex and wisdom to discern what style fits the moment. It transforms leadership from habit into discipline.

The Modes of Influence: Leadership Styles

Leaders influence followers in many ways, but research has identified six primary styles that appear consistently across organizations and cultures. Each has strengths, weaknesses, and contexts where it works best.

The **directive style** is most effective in moments of crisis or when followers lack competence. In emergencies, people do not need consensus they need clarity, order, and fast decisions. During the 2010 Chilean mine disaster, for example, directive leadership was essential. Lives were at stake, and rescue operations required precise coordination and compliance. In such contexts, strong direction saves lives. Yet if a leader continues to use this style in stable environments, it quickly suffocates initiative, erodes trust, and creates a climate of fear.

PART 4 - FOCUS ON THE SITUATION

The **visionary style** thrives when organizations face change or uncertainty. Followers may be skilled and capable, but they need a sense of direction and purpose to sustain their morale. A visionary leader paints the bigger picture and rallies people around it, offering not just tasks but meaning. Visionary leaders cast compelling visions that unite people during times of crisis and uncertainty. His leadership was effective not because he commanded, but because he inspired people to believe in a future larger than themselves.

The **affiliative style** becomes invaluable when teams are strained, trust is broken, or morale is low. At such times, what followers need is not more pressure but more empathy. Leaders who emphasize relationships, care, and human connection can stabilize a fractured organization. After crises, for example, many effective leaders begin by rebuilding trust, creating harmony, and restoring emotional balance before shifting focus back to performance. But if leaders rely exclusively on affiliation, they risk avoiding the difficult conversations and accountability needed for results.

The **democratic style** fits situations where followers are competent, trust is strong, and the leader recognizes that diverse perspectives enrich the decision-making process. Abraham Lincoln's presidency is one of the clearest illustrations. He famously surrounded himself with a "team of rivals," advisors who often disagreed with him. By inviting their input, Lincoln's decisions became sharper and more resilient. However, democratic leadership can slow progress. In urgent situations, seeking consensus may cost valuable time.

The **coaching style** is perhaps the most overlooked in leadership practice but among the most transformative over the long term. Coaching focuses on developing people's capabilities, preparing them for future responsibility, and investing in their growth. It is not the style for crises, but in times of stability it is indispensable. Bill Campbell, known as the "coach of Silicon Valley," exemplified this style. He invested in leaders like Steve Jobs and Eric Schmidt, guiding them not just in business strategy but in personal growth and self-awareness. His legacy demonstrates that coaching creates ripple effects that last for generations of leaders.

Finally, the **pacesetting style** can drive extraordinary results when leading highly motivated and skilled followers. By setting a rapid pace and modeling excellence, the leader challenges others to rise to the standard. Elon Musk often operates in this mode, setting relentless goals and expecting his teams to keep up. This approach can produce groundbreaking innovations but comes at a cost: many teams burn out under the intensity. Pacesetting works best when followers share the same level of motivation and thrive under pressure, but if applied universally it exhausts more than it inspires.

Each style has a place. None is universally effective. The productive leader's role is to assess the situation and choose the style that serves the purpose and the people best.

Integrating Follower Readiness

Leadership style must also be matched to follower readiness, which involves competence, commitment, trust, and reliability. A follower with low competence and low commitment may require a directive style to provide structure and urgency. Someone with moderate competence and growing trust may respond best to a coaching or democratic approach. High competence, reliability, and mutual trust call for visionary or affiliative leadership, while highly motivated and skilled teams can flourish under a pacesetting leader if their energy is sustained.

In reality, leaders rarely use one style exclusively. With one follower, you may be directive; with another, you may coach. The art of leadership lies not in rigid consistency of style, but in consistency of purpose adapting methods while remaining anchored to the mission.

Linking to Levels of Leadership

This adaptability becomes clearer when seen through John Maxwell's Levels of Leadership. At Level 1, where people follow because they must, directive leadership is often unavoidable. At Level 2, where people follow because they want to, affiliative and democratic styles help build trust. At Level 3, where results matter most, visionary and pacesetting leadership prove powerful. At Level 4, where leaders are focused on developing people, coaching becomes central. And at

PART 4 - FOCUS ON THE SITUATION

Level 5, the pinnacle of leadership, the leader seamlessly adapts styles as situations demand, guided not by ego but by purpose.

This shows that leadership styles are not rigid steps to be mastered in order. They are tools a leader learns to use wisely, depending on where they are with their followers and the situation at hand.

Case Study 7
Jacinda Ardern — Adaptive Leadership in Action

On **March 15, 2019**, tragedy struck New Zealand when a terrorist attacked two mosques in Christchurch, killing **51 worshippers** and injuring dozens more. The event shocked one of the world's most peaceful nations and tested its leadership at the deepest human level.

Prime Minister **Jacinda Ardern** demonstrated, in real time, what *adaptive leadership* looks like. Within hours, she moved fluidly across several leadership modes — each calibrated to the situation and the emotional readiness of her people.

- **Directive:** In the immediate aftermath, she acted swiftly to secure the nation, issuing clear emergency orders, coordinating the police response, and communicating accurate information to prevent panic.
- **Affiliative:** Visiting grieving families within days, she led through empathy — wearing a hijab as a gesture of solidarity and personally comforting victims' relatives. Her compassion became a unifying national image.
- **Visionary:** She reframed the tragedy around a shared identity, declaring in Parliament, *"They are us."* That phrase turned division into belonging and gave the nation a healing narrative.
- **Democratic:** Ten days later, she worked across political lines to pass decisive gun-law reforms banning military-style weapons. Collaboration, not partisanship, defined her leadership.

Ardern's conduct illustrated that **adaptive leaders don't change who they are — they change how they lead to meet what people need.** Her clarity ensured safety, her empathy restored dignity, and her vision rekindled unity.

Lesson: Productive leadership is not a single style but the ability to harmonize multiple styles in real time, guided by purpose, compassion, and courage.

Table: Leadership Styles, Situations, and Impact

Style	Best Situation	Risks if Overused	Example Impact on Followers
Directive	Crises, low competence	Fear, disengagement	Provides clarity, order
Visionary	Change, uncertainty	Can ignore details	Inspires purpose, motivates
Affiliative	Low morale, broken trust	Avoids hard truths	Builds harmony, restores trust
Democratic	Competent, trustworthy teams	Slows decisions	Builds ownership, engagement
Coaching	Long-term development	Ineffective in crises	Grows people, builds capacity
Pacesetting	High skill, high motivation	Burnout, resentment	Pushes for excellence, drives results

PART 4 - FOCUS ON THE SITUATION

Exercise 15: Matching Style to Situation

Think of three current challenges you face. For each, reflect on the following:

1. What does this situation demand of me as a leader?

_____

_____

_____

2. Which leadership style will best serve my followers' readiness in this context?

_____

_____

_____

3. Am I willing to adapt my natural style, even if it feels uncomfortable, to serve the purpose better?

_____

_____

_____

The **productive leader** never clings to one style. They carry a full toolkit: directive when urgency calls, visionary when direction fades, affiliative when trust is broken, democratic when wisdom is shared, coaching when growth is needed, and pacesetting when excellence is possible.

What matters most is not *which* style you prefer, but *whether* your style fits the situation and serves the shared purpose.

Adaptive leaders unlock the highest potential in both themselves and those they lead — because they lead not by habit, but by harmony between purpose, people, and situation.

CHAPTER 18

Leading in a VUCA World

"Today's certainty is tomorrow's chaos. The only way to lead effectively is to embrace the unknown and help others navigate it."

— ANONYMOUS

We live in a world defined by **VUCA** — Volatility, Uncertainty, Complexity, and Ambiguity.

Coined by U.S. military strategists after the Cold War, the term now describes the everyday reality of global business and leadership. The world moves faster, systems interconnect more tightly, and change unfolds with greater unpredictability than ever before.

In such an environment, leadership is no longer about control — it is about **orientation and adaptation**. Productive leaders do not attempt to eliminate chaos; they learn to navigate it with resilience, foresight, and calm confidence.

Volatility: When Conditions Swing Wildly

Volatility describes the *speed and turbulence* of change — when yesterday's assumptions no longer hold today.

A vivid example comes from the food-supply chain. In 2025, extreme weather drove global cocoa and coffee prices to double. Droughts in West Africa and floods in South America disrupted harvests, sending shock waves through markets. Analysts warned that unless companies diversified supply sources, volatility would remain the new normal.

Financial markets echo this instability. Inflation pressures and unpredictable trade policies can trigger violent swings within hours. Yet volatility is never random; it is the signal of a system under transformation. Productive leaders treat these fluctuations as information to anticipate, not as chaos to fear.

Uncertainty – When the Future Refuses to Behave

Uncertainty arises when leaders lack reliable information about what lies ahead. Unlike volatility, which is about speed, uncertainty is about *invisibility*.

During 2025, several global companies — including Ford and American Airlines — withdrew forward guidance as shifting tariffs and regulatory changes made forecasts meaningless. Geopolitical tension in Eastern Europe and the Middle East added further fog. In such climates, even seasoned executives admitted: *"We simply don't know what happens next."*

In these conditions, productive leaders focus less on prediction and more on **preparation**. They build flexible strategies, test scenarios, and train their teams to act decisively with incomplete information.

Complexity – When Everything Connects to Everything

Complexity emerges when problems are no longer isolated but woven together in intricate networks. The challenge is not lack of data — it is *too much* data intertwined.

Consider global e-commerce. A single product launch now involves cross-border logistics, real-time analytics, sustainability compliance, and rapidly shifting consumer sentiment. One small change in regulation or public opinion can ripple through the entire system.

Complexity also defines our biggest collective issues — climate, healthcare, digital transformation. No leader or nation can solve them alone. Productive leaders practice **systems thinking**: they step back to see the patterns, simplify priorities, and focus their people on what truly matters.

Ambiguity — When Meaning Itself Is Unclear

Ambiguity exists when information can be interpreted in multiple ways and the "right" path is hidden in the fog.

Artificial intelligence offers a clear illustration. Breakthroughs in automation and productivity are dazzling, but ethical boundaries — privacy, bias, job displacement — remain undefined. Leaders must decide while the rules are still being written.

Ambiguity is not too much data or too little; it is the absence of clear meaning. Productive leaders respond through **experimentation and learning loops** — acting, observing outcomes, and adjusting fast. Progress in ambiguity comes not from certainty, but from curiosity and courage.

Link to the Productive Leadership Model

VUCA does not introduce new leadership principles; it **tests** the existing ones. Productive leaders apply their disciplined loop — **Observe → Interpret → Decide → Act → Learn.**

- **Volatility** tests a leader's **Character** — the calm integrity to stay grounded amid chaos.
- **Uncertainty** tests **Competence** — the ability to make sound judgments with limited data.
- **Complexity** tests **Communication** — the clarity to cut through noise and align people.
- **Ambiguity** tests **Courage** — the willingness to act before full certainty exists.

In this way, VUCA becomes not a threat but the *proving ground* of productive leadership.

PART 4 - FOCUS ON THE SITUATION

From VUCA to VUCA Prime — The Leadership Response

It is not enough to diagnose volatility, uncertainty, complexity, and ambiguity. Leaders must also know how to counter them.

Bob Johansen of the Institute for the Future proposed **VUCA Prime**, a mirror framework that transforms chaos into capability:

VUCA Challenge	Leadership Response	Practical Example
Volatility	**Vision** — Provide a steady beacon of purpose when everything shifts.	Elon Musk's consistent mission "to accelerate the world's transition to sustainable energy" anchors Tesla through wild market swings.
Uncertainty	**Understanding** — Listen broadly, gather intelligence, and sense patterns.	Governments that sought scientific expertise during COVID-19 navigated uncertainty better than those that ignored it.
Complexity	**Clarity** — Simplify priorities and empower small, clear-mission teams.	Jeff Bezos's "two-pizza team" model at Amazon kept decisions fast despite massive scale.
Ambiguity	**Agility** — Experiment, pivot, and learn faster than change itself.	Satya Nadella's agile shift to cloud computing repositioned Microsoft in a still-ambiguous tech future.

VUCA Prime does not eliminate turbulence; it equips leaders to **navigate** it.

Exercise 16: My VUCA Prime

Reflect on your leadership context. For each dimension, write one concrete action you will take this quarter:

1. Where is volatility shaking my world, and what **vision** can I clarify for my people?

_____

_____

2. Where am I facing uncertainty, and how can I deepen my **understanding** before deciding?

_____

_____

3. What complexities overwhelm my team, and how can I bring **clarity**?

_____

_____

4. Where does **ambiguity** slow progress, and how can I act with greater **agility**?

_____

_____

VUCA is real and relentless — but not unbeatable. By responding with **Vision, Understanding, Clarity,** and **Agility**, leaders turn turbulence into transformation.

The productive leader is not paralyzed by disruption; they are **sharpened** by it. In a world that refuses to slow down, the highest form of leadership is not control — it is *composed adaptability.*

CHAPTER 19
Situation Engineering

"The best way to predict the future is to create it."

— PETER DRUCKER

Most leaders spend their time reacting to circumstances as though they are fixed realities beyond their control. But the truth is: leaders can influence, design, and even **engineer situations**.

While no one can dictate external events, every leader can shape the *internal conditions, systems,* and *cultures* in which their people operate.

This proactive mindset is what separates merely adaptive leaders from **productive leaders** — those who lead by design, not by chance.

What Is Situation Engineering?

Situation engineering is the deliberate act of shaping context so that people naturally behave in ways that align with purpose and desired outcomes. It is leadership through design — constructing cultures, systems, incentives, and communication flows that make success predictable rather than accidental.

Reactive leadership asks, *"How do I respond?"*

Productive leadership asks, *"How do I shape the game so my people can win?"*

From Reaction to Design

Reactive leadership waits for problems to appear, then adjusts. Situation engineering, by contrast, means **creating conditions where the likelihood of**

success is built in. Instead of only asking, "How do I respond?" productive leaders also ask, "How do I shape the game so my people can win?"

Consider sports. A great coach does not just react to the opposing team during the match; they design training systems, drills, and culture long before game day. By the time players step onto the field, the "situation" has already been engineered for resilience and performance.

Link to the Productive Leadership Model

Situation Engineering is the *operational face* of productive leadership. Where earlier chapters explored purpose, systems, and people, this chapter shows how leaders fuse them into an ecosystem that drives results.

- They build **clarity of purpose**, so everyone knows *why* they act.
- They create **systems** that make the right behaviors the easiest choice.
- They embed **accountability** through transparency and feedback.
- They sustain **growth** by engineering urgency, learning, and innovation into daily routines.

In essence, Situation Engineering is the *architecture of productivity* — the moment when leadership becomes intentional design.

Case Study 8
Samsung-Manufacturing Crisis for Excellence

In the 1980s, Samsung was viewed as a producer of low-quality, low-cost products. Its CEO at the time, **Lee Byung-chul**, knew this perception would doom the company in the long term. To transform Samsung into a global symbol of quality, he did something extraordinary: he **manufactured a crisis.**

In one famous incident, Samsung publicly destroyed millions of dollars' worth of defective phones and electronics in front of employees. The message was unmistakable: quality was non-negotiable. Lee later explained in an interview: "I manufacture crises to get the results that I want."

By engineering a situation where employees felt the urgency of change even when no external crisis demanded it Samsung shifted its DNA. Within decades, it moved from being a cheap producer to one of the world's leading brands in electronics and smartphones.

Case Study 9
Steve Jobs- Using Crisis to Accelerate Innovation

Steve Jobs also understood the power of engineered situations. During his battle with illness, he used the urgency of his limited time to inspire his team at Apple to deliver extraordinary results. Colleagues recalled how Jobs reminded them that life was short and that they had a window to create products that would change the world.

Within a year, Apple delivered breakthroughs like the iMac and, later, the iPhone. Jobs didn't just lead through personal charisma he **engineered urgency** by turning his illness into a rallying cry for focus, speed, and excellence.

By reframing his personal struggle as a shared moment of purpose, Jobs created a situation in which his followers gave their very best.

Tools of Situation Engineering

Productive leaders engineer situations through multiple levers. The choice of lever depends on the outcome they seek:

- **Culture Design**: Establishing norms that encourage ownership, transparency, and accountability. Netflix engineered a culture of "freedom and responsibility," empowering innovation while maintaining discipline.
- **System and Process Design**: Toyota's lean manufacturing system engineered quality and efficiency into every stage of production, making excellence routine.
- **Incentive Structures**: Aligning rewards with desired behavior. If collaboration matters, incentives must celebrate teamwork, not just individual performance.

- **Information Flow**: Transparency creates clarity; secrecy creates confusion. Leaders engineer situations by shaping how openly information is shared.
- **Manufacturing Urgency**: Like Samsung or Jobs, leaders can create urgency to break complacency and accelerate change.

Situation Engineering is not manipulation; it is *environmental design* that makes the productive path the natural one.

Personal Story

In my current role, I discovered that one of the biggest barriers to productivity was not lack of talent, but lack of **knowledge sharing.** Employees tended to hold on to information, and critical knowledge often remained siloed. This culture made collaboration difficult and slowed down decision-making.

To engineer a better situation, I introduced an **operational excellence model** where people were supported by process and technology. We began building a **process asset library** consisting of policies, procedures, and manuals, fully integrated with Microsoft SharePoint. We also established **Power BI dashboards** that allowed functional and organizational leaders to monitor progress in real time.

This forced all employees to document their work and upload it to SharePoint, making knowledge visible and accessible to those who needed it. For the first time, information was not hidden but shared. Transparency became the default, and dashboards provided accountability. Over time, the culture shifted: instead of hoarding knowledge, employees began to see themselves as stewards of collective intelligence.

By engineering the systems and incentives, we created a situation where knowledge-sharing became unavoidable and productivity followed.

Exercise 17: Engineering My Situation

Choose one recurring problem your team faces. Reflect:

1. What aspects of **culture** are shaping this problem?

_____

_____

2. What **systems or processes** are enabling it?

_____

_____

3. What **incentives** are rewarding the wrong behavior?

_____

_____

4. What changes in **information flow or urgency** could reshape this situation?

_____

_____

Leaders who only react remain prisoners of circumstance.

Leaders who **engineer** situations take ownership of context itself — the invisible stage on which performance unfolds.

They design culture, systems, incentives, and urgency so that productive outcomes become *inevitable*.

As Samsung and Apple proved, sometimes the most transformative act of leadership is not to wait for a crisis, but to **create one with purpose.**

The most productive leaders don't merely adapt to situations — **they shape them.**

CHAPTER 20

Leading Change

"It is not the strongest of the species that survives, nor the most intelligent, but the one most responsive to change."

— CHARLES DARWIN

Change is the leader's permanent companion. Markets shift, technology evolves, expectations rise. In such a world, survival is not about strength or intelligence — it is about adaptability.

Yet productive leaders go further: they don't merely react to change — they **shape it.**

Change Vs. Transformation

Change is the process of moving from one state to another. It may involve new policies, updated systems, or revised strategies. Change can be incremental, reversible, and specific.

Transformation, however, is deeper. Transformation is not just about doing things differently; it is about becoming something different. Where change modifies processes, transformation reshapes identity. For example, a bank switching from manual to digital customer onboarding is changing. A bank reimagining itself as a fintech company that operates like a tech startup is transformation.

The productive leader must understand the difference. Change management keeps organizations efficient. Transformation leadership makes them future

The Change Formula

Why do some change efforts succeed while others fail? Richard Beckhard and David Gleicher developed a simple but powerful insight often called the **Change Formula**:

$$D \times V \times F > R$$

- **Dissatisfaction (D):** People must feel enough pain or frustration with the current state. If everyone is comfortable, they won't move.
- **Vision (V):** A compelling picture of the future must exist. Without vision, dissatisfaction just produces complaint, not action.
- **First Steps (F):** People must know what to do next. Big visions without small steps overwhelm.
- **Resistance (R):** All change meets resistance. For change to succeed, the product of dissatisfaction, vision, and first steps must be greater than the resistance.

This formula explains why many leaders fail. They may have a vision, but no real dissatisfaction. Or they may have dissatisfaction and first steps but no inspiring vision. The formula reminds us that all three must be present, and multiplied not added for change to overcome resistance.

Kotter's 8 Steps of Leading Change

Harvard professor **John Kotter** studied why most organizational change efforts fail. His conclusion: leaders underestimate resistance and overestimate the power of a single announcement. Change is not an event—it is a process. Kotter's eight steps provide a roadmap:

1. **Create Urgency.** Without a sense of urgency, people will not leave their comfort zones. Lee Byung-chul at Samsung manufactured a crisis to jolt people into action. Urgency breaks inertia.
2. **Build a Guiding Coalition.** No leader drives transformation alone. Change requires a committed group of influential people who model

belief and behavior. Successful transformations require allies who embody the vision alongside the leader.

3. **Form a Strategic Vision.** Vision translates urgency into direction. It answers the question: Where are we going? Satya Nadella transformed Microsoft not by fear, but by articulating a growth mindset vision.
4. **Communicate the Vision.** Change dies in silence. Leaders must communicate constantly, consistently, and clearly. Steve Jobs repeated Apple's vision until it was embedded in the culture.
5. **Empower Broad Action.** Barriers structural or cultural must be removed. If systems or incentives block change, no amount of speeches will help. Leaders engineer situations (as we saw in Chapter 19) so people are free to act.
6. **Generate Short-Term Wins.** Long transformations exhaust people without visible results. Leaders must design early victories quick wins that prove progress is possible. These wins build momentum and silence skeptics.
7. **Sustain Acceleration.** After the first wins, complacency creeps back. Leaders must build on momentum, push for more ambitious changes, and remind people that transformation is not over.
8. **Institute Change.** Finally, new behaviors must become part of the culture. If change is not embedded in values, norms, and systems, people will eventually revert to old ways. True transformation is only complete when it feels like "the way we do things around here."

Link to the Productive Leadership Model

Leading change is the ultimate test of **productive leadership**:

Productive Leadership Element	Expression in Change
Purpose	Defines *why* change matters — the emotional anchor amid uncertainty.
Systems	Translate vision into repeatable routines and visible progress.

People	Engage followers as partners, not passengers, in shaping the future.
Results	Ensure transformation produces measurable, positive impact.

Where adaptive leaders react to external shifts, productive leaders **design internal momentum** — aligning purpose, systems, people, and results so that change becomes self-sustaining.

Personal Story

In my current role, I encountered major resistance to change rooted in culture. People were comfortable with established ways of working, even when they were inefficient. Instead of simply issuing directives, I applied elements of the change formula and Kotter's model.

We started by **creating dissatisfaction** with the status quo highlighting financial penalties we were paying due to outdated processes. At the same time, I introduced a **compelling vision** of operational excellence: a workplace where knowledge was shared, data was visible, and accountability was transparent.

We then took **first steps** by building a process asset library in SharePoint, creating Power BI dashboards, and making information accessible. These changes became early **short-term wins** suddenly, leaders could see real-time data on compliance and performance.

Resistance did not vanish, but by engineering urgency, showing wins, and communicating vision repeatedly, the culture began to shift. Over time, what once felt like radical change became normal practice.

Exercise 18: Applying the Change Formula

Think of one change you are leading (or need to lead). Reflect:

1. How strong is dissatisfaction with the current state?

_____

_____

2. How compelling is the vision of the future?

_____

_____

3. What first steps are clear and actionable?

_____

_____

4. What forms of resistance do I anticipate and how will I address them?

_____

_____

Change is inevitable. Transformation is intentional.

Productive leaders don't merely endure disruption — they **orchestrate it**.

By combining **urgency, vision, small wins, and sustained systems**, they turn resistance into momentum and chaos into clarity.

They engineer environments where change becomes culture — where tomorrow's transformation is simply *today's normal.*

PART 4 - FOCUS ON THE SITUATION

Part 4: Summary

Leadership does not happen in isolation; it unfolds within a constantly changing environment. In this part, productive leadership evolves from guiding people to mastering **context** — the ability to read, adapt to, and shape situations for purposeful outcomes.

Chapter 15 introduces situational awareness — the discipline of diagnosing external forces, internal conditions, and follower readiness before acting. Chapter 16 expands this into structured assessment, helping leaders turn perception into insight. In Chapter 17, leaders learn to match their style to the situation, shifting fluidly between directive, visionary, affiliative, democratic, coaching, and pacesetting modes based on need, not preference.

Chapter 18 explores leadership in a **VUCA world**, where volatility, uncertainty, complexity, and ambiguity redefine success. Productive leaders respond with **Vision, Understanding, Clarity, and Agility**, turning turbulence into opportunity. Chapter 19 advances this thinking with **Situation Engineering** — designing culture, systems, incentives, and urgency so that excellence becomes inevitable. Finally, Chapter 20 focuses on **Leading Change**, transforming resistance into momentum through vision, urgency, and disciplined execution.

Together, these chapters show that productive leadership is not reactive but **intentional by design**. True leaders don't merely survive their situations — they **read, shape, and transform** them to align purpose, people, and systems toward lasting results.

PART 5
TOOLS FOR PRODUCTIVE LEADERSHIP

PART 5 - TOOLS FOR PRODUCTIVE LEADERSHIP

Part 5: Introduction

> *"A bad system will beat a good person every time."*
> W. EDWARDS DEMING

Leadership is often described as an art, but it is also a discipline. And like any discipline, it benefits from tools. Just as a surgeon uses precise instruments to operate, or an engineer relies on models to solve problems, leaders need tools that make the invisible visible, the complex simple, and the abstract actionable.

Why Leaders Need Tools

Instincts are inconsistent and charisma fades under pressure. Tools create **structure**. They help leaders clarify problems, align teams, and track progress. A productive leader does not only inspire they equip themselves and their teams with instruments that sharpen thinking, reduce ambiguity, and drive execution. Tools make leadership **repeatable, teachable, and scalable**.

How to Use These Tools

Leadership tools are not checklists to tick off. They are **thinking aids** that must be:

- Adapted to context, not adopted blindly.
- Used collaboratively to create shared language.
- Linked to action so they inspire behavior change.

Systems Matter

Tools without systems are one-off exercises. A leadership system integrates tools into the daily rhythm of planning, execution, and review. Systems ensure that leadership is **consistent, measurable, and sustainable**.

Introducing the Toolkit

This part of the book provides **17 practical tools** that leaders can carry into boardrooms, workshops, and coaching conversations.

- **Leader Tools** : Frameworks and diagnostics to build self-awareness (e.g., Productive Leadership Canvas, Leadership Style Assessments, 5C Questionnaire).
- **Follower Tools** : Instruments to assess readiness, courage, and autonomy (e.g., Follower Readiness, Courageous Follower Assessment, Autonomy Spectrum).
- **Situation Tools** : Lenses for navigating complexity and turbulence (e.g., Style–Situation Grid, VUCA Prime Lens, Change Leadership Roadmap).
- **Systems & Growth Tools** : Scorecards and development plans to sustain productivity (e.g., Leadership Productivity Scorecard, Leadership Development Plan).

Each tool connects back to the book's central thesis: **leadership is not who you are, but what happens between leaders, followers, and situations.**

Tool 1: The 10 Keys to Productive Leadership Framework

Purpose

To define productive leadership in a way that is **simple, powerful, and actionable**. This version uses a consistent sentence structure, so leaders can **remember, repeat, and practice** the 10 Keys easily.

The 10 Keys to Productive Leadership

1. **Productive Leadership is a Process**: it happens between the leader, the followers, and the situation, not in isolation.
2. **Productive Leadership Has Purpose** : it begins with a clear "why" that inspires direction and meaning.
3. **Productive Leadership Stands on Values** : it is anchored in integrity, principles, and what a leader is willing to sacrifice for.
4. **Productive Leadership Builds Vision** : it paints a compelling picture of the future that unites people.
5. **Productive Leadership Uses Influence Wisely** : it draws from multiple sources of power to guide, not control.
6. **Productive Leadership Adapts Style** : it flexes its approach based on followers' readiness and situational demands.
7. **Productive Leadership Engages Followers** : it empowers people to take ownership and share in the purpose.
8. **Productive Leadership Designs Systems** : it establishes structures, processes, and tools that sustain performance.
9. **Productive Leadership Delivers Results** : it is measured by impact, accountability, and outcomes that matter.
10. **Productive Leadership Grows Continuously** : it invests in learning, renewal, and development of self, others, and the organization.

PART 5 - TOOLS FOR PRODUCTIVE LEADERSHIP

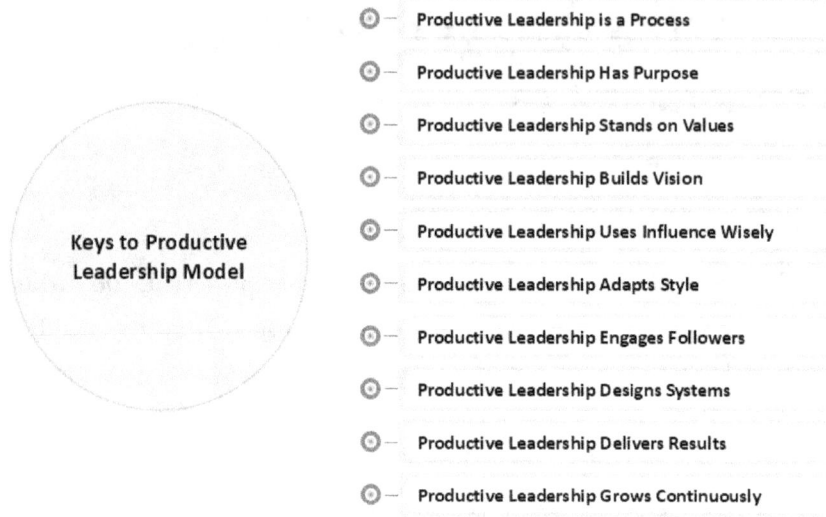

Figure 13: Keys to Productive Leadership

How to Use This Tool

- **Memorize** the 10 sentences they form your leadership creed.
- **Recite** them in team meetings to keep leadership front of mind.
- **Assess** yourself monthly against each key.
- **Anchor** every tool in this Part back to one of the 10 sentences.

Reflection Exercise

Which of these 10 sentences resonates most with me today?

_____

Which one challenges me the most?

_____

What will I do this week to embody that key?

_____

Tool 2: The Productive Leadership Canvas

Purpose

The Productive Leadership Canvas is the **most important tool of this book**. It provides a **one-page visual framework** that helps leaders integrate the three core elements of leadership **Leader, Followers, and Situation** around a shared **Purpose & Outcomes**.

This canvas transforms leadership from abstract concepts into a **practical map** that can be filled in, revisited, and used as a guide for daily practice.

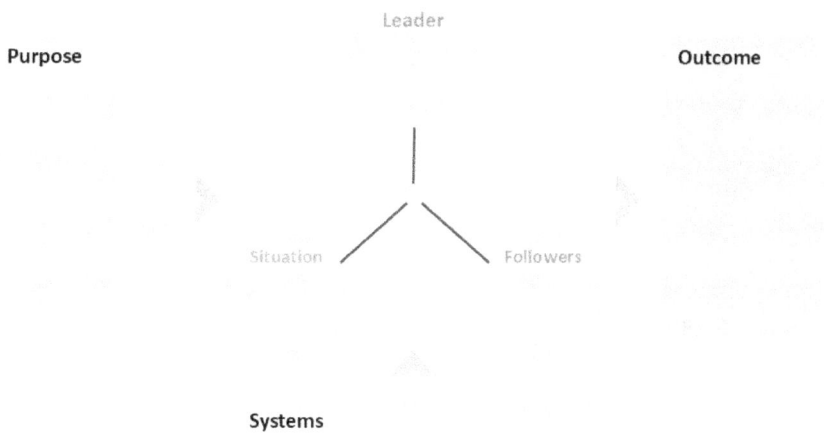

Figure 14: Productive Leadership Canvas

- **Leader:** Assess your values, leadership style, energy, and sources of influence.
- **Followers:** Identify readiness, trust, reliability, engagement, and courageous followership behaviors.

- **Situation:** Diagnose the environment stable, uncertain, volatile, complex, or in crisis.
- **Systems & Tools:** List processes, structures, and scorecards that support or limit productivity.
- **Purpose & Outcomes:** Define your *Why* and agree on success measures that unify all quadrants.

How to Complete the Canvas

1. **Step 1 – Leader:** Write down your personal values, default leadership style, and key sources of power. Ask yourself: *Am I using influence beyond position?*
2. **Step 2 – Followers:** Map your team's strengths, readiness levels, and level of trust/reliability. Identify who needs support, who is ready for empowerment.
3. **Step 3 – Situation:** Note the external and internal context. Is your team in a high-change environment? Are you dealing with crises, competition, or uncertainty?
4. **Step 4 – Systems & Tools:** List the systems (e.g., dashboards, policies, procedures) that exist. Do they enable or block productivity?
5. **Step 5 – Purpose & Outcomes:** Write a clear, inspiring purpose. Define 3–5 success metrics that connect leader, followers, and situation into one aligned direction.

How to Use the Canvas

- **Diagnostic Tool:** Use at the start of any project, leadership cycle, or transformation.
- **Alignment Tool:** Complete it together with your team to ensure alignment around purpose.
- **Review Tool:** Revisit quarterly to see what has shifted update leader behaviors, follower readiness, situation context, and systems.
- **Communication Tool:** Use it to brief stakeholders, boards, or teams so leadership decisions are transparent and evidence-based.

Reflection Exercise

What did I learn about myself when filling in the Leader quadrant?
_____

Which followers surprised me most in terms of readiness or reliability?
_____

What systems must I strengthen or redesign to support productivity?
_____

How clearly have I defined Purpose & Outcomes for my team?
_____

Tool 3: Leader Self-Assessment Diagnostic

Purpose

Productive leadership begins with **self-awareness**. Leaders must be able to look inward before they can lead outward. This tool gives you a **structured questionnaire** to reflect on your own values, energy, influence, and accountability.

By answering these questions honestly, you will see patterns in your leadership strengths to leverage and blind spots to address.

The Questionnaire

Values & Integrity

What principles guide my decisions, even when they cost me personally or professionally?

_____

Do I consistently practice what I preach? Give one example where I did, and one where I fell short.

_____

What am I willing to give up to stay true to my values?

_____

Energy & Presence

Do I energize or drain people when I walk into a room?

_____

Am I setting the "weather" of my team in a positive or negative way?

_____

What habits help me stay grounded and positive under pressure?

___

Influence & Power

Beyond my job title, what are my true sources of influence? (e.g., expertise, relationships, vision, credibility)

___

When was the last time I was influenced without using my position?

___

Do I rely too much on authority? How can I use other sources of power?

___

Results & Accountability

Am I focused more on activities or outcomes? Give an example.

___

Do I hold myself accountable as much as I hold others accountable?

___

When things go wrong, do I own responsibility or shift blame?

___

How to Complete This Tool

1. Set aside 30–45 minutes of uninterrupted time.
2. Answer each question honestly in writing.
3. Highlight 2 answers you are proud of and 2 answers that reveal a gap.
4. Share one insight with a trusted colleague or mentor to gain perspective.

PART 5 - TOOLS FOR PRODUCTIVE LEADERSHIP

How to Use This Tool

- **Quarterly Self-Check:** Repeat every 3 months to track your growth.
- **Coaching Aid:** Share with a coach/mentor to guide your leadership development plan.
- **Team Dialogue:** Discuss selected answers with your team to build trust and accountability.

Reflection Exercise

The one thing I learned about myself from this diagnostic:

_____

One area I will intentionally improve in the next 30 days:

_____

Tool 4: Leadership Style Self-Assessment

Purpose

Leadership is not "one-size-fits-all." Every leader has a **natural style** a way they default to leading under normal conditions. This self-assessment helps you discover **which leadership style you lean toward most**, so that you can recognize your strengths, acknowledge your risks, and begin to adapt flexibly.

The Questionnaire

Instructions: Read each statement and rate yourself on a scale of **1–5**:
1 = Strongly Disagree   2 = Disagree   3 = Neutral   4 = Agree   5 = Strongly Agree

Directive (Authoritative)

1. I prefer to set clear rules and expect them to be followed. [1–5]
2. I take charge quickly when decisions need to be made. [1–5]
3. In a crisis, I prefer giving orders to maintain control. [1–5]
4. I am most comfortable when I know others are following my direction. [1–5]

Democratic (Participative)

1. I regularly involve my team in decision-making. [1–5]
2. I value diverse opinions, even if it slows the process. [1–5]
3. I build consensus before moving forward on major issues. [1–5]
4. I prefer when decisions reflect group input rather than my own view alone. [1–5]

Coaching

1. I spend time developing people rather than just directing them. [1–5]
2. I see mistakes as opportunities for growth. [1–5]

3. I invest energy in understanding each person's strengths and weaknesses. [1–5]
4. I feel most successful when my people grow into stronger leaders. [1–5]

Visionary (Transformational)

1. I communicate a compelling vision of the future. [1–5]
2. I inspire people with meaning and purpose. [1–5]
3. I challenge the status quo and push for innovation. [1–5]
4. People often look to me for inspiration and motivation. [1–5]

Affiliative

1. I focus on creating harmony and connection in my team. [1–5]
2. I am empathetic and care deeply about how people feel. [1–5]
3. I step in to heal conflict and restore relationships. [1–5]
4. I believe people work best when they feel supported and included. [1–5]

Pacesetting

1. I set very high standards for myself and others. [1–5]
2. I expect people to keep up with my intensity and pace. [1–5]
3. I often lead by example, working harder than anyone else. [1–5]
4. I can become impatient when people don't perform at my level. [1–5]

Laissez-Faire (Delegative)

1. I trust people to make their own decisions without my interference. [1–5]
2. I step back once I assign responsibility. [1–5]
3. I am comfortable giving wide autonomy to capable individuals. [1–5]
4. I encourage independence and self-management in my team. [1–5]

Scoring

- Add up your scores for each style:
    - Directive: Q1–4
    - Democratic: Q5–8

- Coaching: Q9–12
- Visionary: Q13–16
- Affiliative: Q17–20
- Pacesetting: Q21–24
- Laissez-Faire: Q25–28

Highest score = your natural style
Second highest = your backup style
Lowest score = your blind spot

How to Interpret

- **Directive:** Strong in crises, but may create passive followers if overused.
- **Democratic:** Builds buy-in, but risks slow decisions in urgent contexts.
- **Coaching:** Grows people for the long-term, but may delay short-term results.
- **Visionary:** Inspires transformation, but must be balanced with execution.
- **Affiliative:** Builds trust and morale, but risks avoiding accountability.
- **Pacesetting:** Drives high performance, but risks follower burnout.
- **Laissez-Faire:** Works with capable, disciplined teams, but can lead to drift without accountability.

How to Use This Tool

1. **Complete the Questionnaire:** Rate yourself honestly.
2. **Tally Your Scores:** Identify your strongest and weakest styles.
3. **Reflect on Risks:** For your top style, ask: *What is the downside if I overuse this?*
4. **Plan for Flexibility:** Commit to practicing one underused style in the coming month.
5. **Link Forward:** Use this baseline to prepare for **Tool 5 (Follower Readiness Questionnaire)** and **Tool 6 (Situation Complexity Questionnaire)**, which will help you know *when* to flex your style.

PART 5 - TOOLS FOR PRODUCTIVE LEADERSHIP

Reflection Exercise

My strongest leadership style is:

_____

My weakest leadership style is:

_____

One way I will expand my range this month is:

_____

Tool 5: Follower Readiness Questionnaire

Purpose

Leadership is only half the equation. The **quality of followers determines the quality of leadership.** Some followers need close guidance, others thrive on autonomy. Leaders must know *where each follower stands today* in order to choose the right leadership style tomorrow.

The **Follower Readiness Questionnaire** measures a follower's **competence, trust, and reliability** to reveal their readiness level.

The Questionnaire

Instructions: For each follower, rate the statements below on a scale of **1–5**:

1 = Strongly Disagree   2 = Disagree   3 = Neutral   4 = Agree   5 = Strongly Agree

Competence (Skills & Knowledge)

1. This follower consistently demonstrates the technical skills required for their role. [1–5]
2. This follower understands how their work contributes to team goals. [1–5]
3. This follower can handle new or complex tasks with minimal supervision. [1–5]

Trust (Character & Integrity)

1. I trust this follower to act ethically and responsibly. [1–5]
2. This follower owns up to mistakes instead of hiding them. [1–5]
3. This follower demonstrates alignment with the organization's values. [1–5]

Reliability (Consistency & Accountability)

1. This follower delivers on time and keeps commitments. [1–5]
2. I can rely on this follower under pressure or in a crisis. [1–5]
3. This follower is consistent in both effort and results. [1–5]

Scoring

- Add up the scores for each dimension:
  - **Competence:** Q1–3 (max 15)
  - **Trust:** Q4–6 (max 15)
  - **Reliability:** Q7–9 (max 15)

Total Readiness Score (max 45): _____

Interpretation:

- **High (35–45):** Ready for empowerment (Supportive, Delegative, Visionary styles).
- **Medium (25–34):** Needs a balance of support and guidance (Coaching, Democratic styles).
- **Low (15–24):** Needs close direction and oversight (Directive or Pacesetting styles).

How to Interpret Results

1. **High Competence + High Trust + High Reliability** → Delegate with confidence.
2. **High Competence + Low Trust** → Monitor ethics/character closely, empower gradually.
3. **Low Competence + High Trust/Reliability** → Coach and develop skills.
4. **Low Across All Dimensions** → Step in with Directive leadership until growth occurs.

How to Use This Tool

1. Complete this questionnaire for **each direct report** at least quarterly.
2. Plot each follower on a readiness spectrum (Low → Medium → High).
3. Compare results across your team identify who needs coaching, who needs autonomy, and who needs closer direction.
4. Use these results to prepare for **Tool 7: Leadership Style–Situation Matching Grid**.

Reflection Exercise

Which follower scored highest in readiness?

_____

Which follower scored lowest in readiness?

_____

How will I adapt my leadership approach to each of them?

_____

Tool 6: Situation Complexity Questionnaire

Purpose

Leadership style is not only shaped by the leader and the followers it is also dictated by the **situation**. A stable environment calls for different leadership than a crisis, just as a complex problem requires a different approach than a routine task.

The **Situation Complexity Questionnaire** helps leaders quickly diagnose whether they are facing a **Stable, Uncertain, Complex, or Crisis** situation. This clarity allows them to choose the **right leadership style** instead of defaulting to habit.

The Questionnaire

Instructions: For your current project, team, or organizational challenge, rate each statement on a scale of **1–5**:

1 = Strongly Disagree   2 = Disagree   3 = Neutral   4 = Agree   5 = Strongly Agree

Clarity of Environment

1. The goals of this situation are clearly defined and understood. [1–5]
2. Roles and responsibilities are well-structured. [1–5]
3. The operating environment is stable and predictable. [1–5]

Urgency & Pressure

1. This situation requires fast action without delay. [1–5]
2. Mistakes would have serious or immediate consequences. [1–5]
3. The stakes are high, with limited room for experimentation. [1–5]

Complexity of Work

1. The situation involves multiple moving parts or stakeholders. [1–5]
2. There are competing priorities and interdependencies. [1–5]
3. The problem requires creativity and problem-solving, not just routine execution. [1–5]

Uncertainty & Change

1. The situation is affected by unknowns or changing external factors. [1–5]
2. There is limited or conflicting information available. [1–5]
3. Plans may need to change rapidly as events unfold. [1–5]

Scoring

- **Stable (Mostly 1–2):** Goals are clear, environment predictable. Best styles: *Democratic, Coaching, Affiliative.*
- **Uncertain (Mix of 2–3):** Some ambiguity, but manageable. Best styles: *Supportive, Democratic, Visionary (for clarity).*
- **Complex (Mostly 3–4):** Many moving parts, interdependencies. Best styles: *Visionary (for direction), Coaching (for growth).*
- **Crisis (Mostly 4–5):** Urgent, high stakes, no room for error. Best styles: *Directive, Pacesetting (short-term).*

How to Interpret Results

- **Stable Situations** → Engage followers, build consensus, and invest in long-term development.
- **Uncertain Situations** → Provide reassurance and clarity, invite participation, and reduce ambiguity.
- **Complex Situations** → Inspire with vision, align multiple stakeholders, and encourage innovation.
- **Crisis Situations** → Take control, decide quickly, and ensure discipline but don't stay in crisis mode longer than necessary.

How to Use This Tool

1. Complete this questionnaire at the start of any major initiative.
2. Reassess regularly in fast-moving environments situations can shift from *Stable* to *Crisis* quickly.
3. Share results with your leadership team to align style and approach.
4. Use the output to prepare for **Tool 7: Leadership Style–Situation Matching Grid**.

Reflection Exercise

The current situation I am facing is best described as:
_____

The leadership style I believe this situation requires is:
_____

One adjustment I will make in my approach today is:
_____

Tool 7: Leadership Style, Situation Matching Grid

Purpose

Leadership becomes **productive** when leaders apply the **right style at the right time**. The Matching Grid is designed to help you integrate three dimensions:

1. **Your Default Style** (Tool 4: Leadership Style Self-Assessment)
2. **Follower Readiness** (Tool 5: Follower Readiness Questionnaire)
3. **Situation Complexity** (Tool 6: Situation Complexity Questionnaire)

By aligning these three, you can consciously choose the style that maximizes impact, instead of relying on habit or preference.

Figure 15: Leadership Style–Situation Matching Grid

Low Readiness Followers + Crisis Situation

- **Best Styles:** Directive, Pacesetting
- **Why:** Followers need clarity, structure, and decisiveness. Crisis demands speed.

Low Readiness Followers + Stable Situation

- **Best Styles:** Coaching, Directive
- **Why:** Use directive to provide initial guidance, but emphasize coaching to build competence.

High Readiness Followers + Crisis Situation

- **Best Styles:** Directive (short-term), Visionary (motivate resilience)
- **Why:** Skilled followers can act independently, but in urgent moments, decisive direction still matters.

High Readiness Followers + Stable Situation

- **Best Styles:** Delegative, Democratic, Affiliative
- **Why:** Empower capable followers, involve them in decisions, and maintain harmony.

High Complexity / Uncertain Situations (Regardless of Readiness)

- **Best Styles:** Visionary (to give meaning and direction), Democratic (to gather insights), Coaching (to prepare people for ambiguity).

How to Complete the Grid

1. **Step 1 – Identify Your Style:** From Tool 4, note your natural and secondary styles.
2. **Step 2 – Assess Followers:** From Tool 5, map each follower as Low, Medium, or High readiness.
3. **Step 3 – Diagnose Situation:** From Tool 6, define whether it is Stable, Uncertain, Complex, or Crisis.

4. **Step 4 – Match:** Use the grid to select the leadership style that best aligns with the intersection of follower readiness and situational complexity.
5. **Step 5 – Flex:** If your default style doesn't fit, commit to flexing into the style that does.

How to Use This Tool

- **One-on-One:** For each direct report, plot readiness vs. situation → choose your approach.
- **Team Planning:** Map the collective readiness of your team to adjust style across the group.
- **Leadership Growth:** Practice styles outside your comfort zone when situations call for them.
- **Coaching Leaders:** Use this grid in workshops to role-play leadership responses in different scenarios.

Reflection Exercise

My default style (from Tool 4) is

_____

One situation where my default style may NOT be the best fit is

_____

The style I will consciously practice in that situation is

_____

Tool 8: Stress Drivers Diagnostic

Purpose

When leaders or followers are under pressure, they unconsciously fall into **stress drivers** automatic patterns that influence how they act and react. These drivers can boost productivity or create friction, especially when leader and follower drivers clash (e.g., a "Hurry Up" leader may overwhelm a "Be Perfect" follower).

This diagnostic reveals your dominant stress driver and helps you manage it consciously, while also understanding how it impacts your team.

The Questionnaire

For each question, choose the option (a, b, c, d, or e) that best reflects how you usually behave, especially under stress.

1. When I have too much to do at once, I tend to…

    a) Focus on getting everything right.
    b) Try to do it all as fast as possible.
    c) Focus on what others expect of me.
    d) Stay strong and not show stress.
    e) Keep trying harder until it's done.

2. When I receive criticism, I usually…

    a) Worry about not being perfect.
    b) Rush to fix things quickly.
    c) Feel bad about letting people down.
    d) Hide my feelings and act unaffected.
    e) Push myself to work harder.

3. When I'm part of a team project, I…

    a) Insist on accuracy and high standards.

PART 5 - TOOLS FOR PRODUCTIVE LEADERSHIP

b) Want to move faster than others.

c) Try to please and get along with everyone.

d) Take on the tough parts without complaint.

e) Show I'm working hard, even if results are unclear.

4. Under pressure, I tend to...

   a) Spend extra time checking details.

   b) Get impatient if things move slowly.

   c) Put others' needs before mine.

   d) Pretend I'm fine, even if I'm not.

   e) Focus on effort more than results.

5. What motivates me most at work is...

   a) Getting things perfect.

   b) Getting things done fast.

   c) Being liked and appreciated.

   d) Being strong and dependable.

   e) Showing I'm trying my hardest.

Scoring

- Each a = Be Perfect
- Each b = Hurry Up
- Each c = Please People
- Each d = Be Strong
- Each e = Try Hard

Step 1: Count how many times you chose each letter.

Step 2: The style with the **highest count** is your **dominant stress driver**.

Step 3: The style with the **second highest count** is your **backup driver**.

Explanation of Drivers

- **Be Perfect** : You value accuracy and high standards. Risk: you may frustrate "Hurry Up" types with your need for detail.
- **Hurry Up** : You value speed and urgency. Risk: you may stress "Be Perfect" types who want to slow down.
- **Please People** : You value harmony and inclusion. Risk: you may avoid hard truths or accountability.
- **Be Strong** : You value strength and resilience. Risk: you may seem distant or unapproachable.
- **Try Hard** : You value effort and persistence. Risk: you may exhaust yourself or others without achieving results.

How to Use This Tool

1. Complete the Test honestly.
2. Identify Your Driver reflect on how it shapes your behavior under stress.
3. Compare Across Your Team ask followers to complete the test too.
    - Example: If you're a Hurry Up leader and they're Be Perfect, you'll both need to adjust expectations.
4. Balance the Drivers talk openly with your team about how stress drivers show up and agree on ways to respect differences.

Reflection Exercise

My dominant stress driver is

_____

This driver stresses others when I:

_____

One way I will manage my driver better with my team is

_____

Tool 9: Energy & Presence Tracker

Purpose

Leaders don't just manage tasks they set the **emotional climate** for their teams. Your energy influences whether people feel drained, connected, or inspired. The **Energy & Presence Tracker** helps you monitor your daily impact so you can consciously create a positive and productive environment.

Framework: The Three Energies

- **Consumable Energy:** Energy that is **used up** through conflict, drama, gossip, or negativity. It drains productivity.
- **Connected Energy**: Energy that flows through collaboration, problem-solving, and teamwork. It sustains productivity.
- **Magnetic Energy** : Energy that **inspires and attracts** others. It comes from vision, passion, and purpose. It multiplies productivity.

How to Complete the Tracker

1. At the end of each day, reflect on your interactions and score yourself:
    - **Consumable Energy:** How often did I allow drama, gossip, or negative emotions to dominate?
    - **Connected Energy:** How much did I foster teamwork and collaboration?
    - **Magnetic Energy:** Did I inspire my team with vision, clarity, or encouragement?
2. Use a simple scale (0–5) for each:
    - 0 = Not at all
    - 5 = Very strong presence
3. Note one example for each type of energy.

Example Daily Tracker

Energy Type	Score (0–5)	Example from Today
Consumable Energy	2	Allowed frustration in a meeting to escalate
Connected Energy	4	Facilitated collaboration between functions
Magnetic Energy	3	Shared vision of project's long-term impact

How to Use This Tool

- **Self-Awareness:** Track your scores daily or weekly to see patterns in how you "set the weather."
- **Team Dialogue:** Invite your team to give you feedback on the energy you bring.
- **Coaching Tool:** Use with a coach to balance your energy profile.
- **Growth Plan:** Aim to reduce **consumable energy** and increase **connected** and **magnetic energy** over time.

Reflection Exercise

What kind of energy did I bring most often this week?

_____

When did I allow consumable energy to dominate?

_____

One step I will take tomorrow to increase connected or magnetic energy:

_____

Tool 10: Values-to-Behavior Alignment Tool

Purpose

Values are the **foundation of leadership** but too often, they remain as words on posters or websites. Productive leaders translate values into **visible behaviors** that their teams can see, feel, and measure.

The **Values-to-Behavior Alignment Tool** helps leaders close the gap between what they believe and what they actually do.

Framework

For each value, identify:

1. **Value Statement** : The principle you claim to live by.
2. **Aligned Behavior** : How that value looks in action.
3. **Evidence** : How others can see or measure it.
4. **Risk of Misalignment** : What happens if you fail to live it.

How to Complete the Tool

1. List your **top 3–5 leadership values** (e.g., Integrity, Service, Accountability, innovation).
2. For each value, define a specific **daily behavior** that demonstrates it.
3. Identify how others will **see the behavior in action**.
4. Write down the **risk** if you don't act on that value.

PART 5 - TOOLS FOR PRODUCTIVE LEADERSHIP

Example Table

Value	Behavior in Action	Evidence Others See	Risk of Misalignment
Integrity	Admit mistakes openly	I acknowledge errors in meetings	Loss of trust, blame culture
Service	Put people first in decision-making	I ask "how will this affect the team?"	Followers feel neglected or exploited
Accountability	Deliver on promises	I meet deadlines consistently	Seen as unreliable, lowers team standards
Innovation	Encourage experimentation	I reward new ideas, even if they fail	Culture of fear, missed opportunities

How to Use This Tool

- **Personal Reflection:** Use as a quarterly self-check are my values visible in my daily leadership?
- **Team Dialogue:** Share with your team and invite them to define team-wide values → behaviors.
- **Performance Management:** Use values and behaviors in coaching, appraisals, and recognition.
- **Culture Building:** Cascade this tool across the organization to create a culture of lived values.

Reflection Exercise

One value I want to live more visibly is

_____

The behavior that will demonstrate this is

_____

The risk if I fail to live this value is

_____

Tool 11: The 5C Leadership Self-Assessment

Purpose

The **5C Model of Leadership** (Character, Competence, Courage, Communication, Commitment) provides a holistic lens to evaluate leadership effectiveness. This tool gives leaders a structured **self-assessment questionnaire** to reflect on these five dimensions and see where they are strongest and where they need growth.

The Questionnaire

Instructions: For each statement, rate yourself on a scale of **1–5**: 1 = Strongly Disagree   2 = Disagree   3 = Neutral   4 = Agree   5 = Strongly Agree

Character (Integrity & Values)

1. I consistently act in alignment with my personal and organizational values. [1–5]
2. I take responsibility for mistakes rather than shifting blame. [1–5]
3. People can rely on me to do the right thing, even when it's difficult. [1–5]

Competence (Skills & Knowledge)

1. I have the expertise needed to lead effectively in my current role. [1–5]
2. I stay updated with new knowledge, trends, and skills relevant to my work. [1–5]
3. My team respects me for the depth of knowledge and judgment I bring. [1–5]

Courage (Boldness & Risk-Taking)

1. I speak up when something is wrong, even if it's unpopular. [1–5]
2. I take calculated risks to drive growth or innovation. [1–5]
3. I stand firm in my convictions under pressure. [1–5]

PART 5 - TOOLS FOR PRODUCTIVE LEADERSHIP

Communication (Clarity & Listening)

1. I clearly articulate vision, goals, and expectations to my team. [1–5]
2. I actively listen and make people feel heard. [1–5]
3. I communicate difficult or uncomfortable messages when needed. [1–5]

Commitment (Dedication & Follow-Through)

1. I deliver on promises, even when it requires extra effort. [1–5]
2. I model consistency and perseverance to my team. [1–5]
3. I put the success of the mission above personal convenience. [1–5]

Scoring

- Add your total for each "C" (Character, Competence, Courage, Communication, Commitment).
- Maximum per "C" = 15 points.
- Circle your highest and lowest.

How to Interpret

- **Character:** If this is high → You are trusted. If low → Focus on integrity, consistency, and trust-building.
- **Competence:** If this is high → You are respected. If low → Invest in learning and skill-building.
- **Courage:** If this is high → You are bold. If low → Work on confidence, risk-taking, and standing firm.
- **Communication:** If this is high → You are clear. If low → Improve listening, clarity, and feedback.
- **Commitment:** If this is high → You are dependable. If low → Strengthen follow-through and perseverance.

How to Use This Tool

1. Complete the questionnaire honestly.
2. Highlight your strongest "C" — leverage it as your leadership anchor.
3. Identify your weakest "C" — build a development plan to strengthen it.
4. Revisit this tool annually to measure growth across the five dimensions.

Reflection Exercise

My strongest "C" is:

_____

My weakest "C" is:

_____

One step I will take this month to strengthen my weakest "C" is:

_____

Tool 12: Courageous Follower Assessment

Purpose

Followers are not passive recipients of leadership they are active participants. Great followers demonstrate **courage**: to support, to challenge, and to take responsibility.

The **Courageous Follower Assessment** helps leaders evaluate how their followers engage with them across five dimensions, and helps followers self-assess their own courage.

Framework: The Five Dimensions of Courageous Followership

1. **Courage to Assume Responsibility** : Taking initiative instead of waiting for instructions.
2. **Courage to Serve** : Supporting the leader and team fully, even in tough times.
3. **Courage to Challenge** : Speaking up respectfully when the leader is wrong.
4. **Courage to Participate in Transformation** : Engaging actively in change and improvement.
5. **Courage to Take Moral Action** : Standing for values, even when it's risky.

The Questionnaire

Instructions: Rate each statement for yourself or for a follower on a scale of **1–5**:

1 = Strongly Disagree   2 = Disagree   3 = Neutral   4 = Agree   5 = Strongly Agree

PART 5 - TOOLS FOR PRODUCTIVE LEADERSHIP

Assume Responsibility
1. I take initiative without waiting for instructions. [1–5]
2. I see myself as accountable for results, not just tasks. [1–5]

Serve
1. I put the needs of the mission and team above personal convenience. [1–5]
2. I support my leader, especially during challenging times. [1–5]

Challenge
1. I speak up respectfully if I believe my leader is making a mistake. [1–5]
2. I raise concerns even when it feels uncomfortable. [1–5]

Participate in Transformation
1. I engage actively in change initiatives instead of resisting them. [1–5]
2. I contribute ideas to improve processes or culture. [1–5]

Take Moral Action
1. I act according to values, even when it could have negative consequences for me. [1–5]
2. I will not follow instructions that I believe are unethical. [1–5]

Scoring
- Add scores for each dimension (2 questions each, max 10 points).
- The dimension with the highest score = follower's strength.
- The lowest score = area for growth.

How to Interpret
- **High Responsibility + High Service:** Dependable, proactive contributor.
- **High Challenge + High Moral Action:** A principled truth-teller valuable but may be difficult to manage.
- **High Transformation:** A change agent, driving innovation.
- **Low in several areas:** May be disengaged or fearful; requires coaching and trust-building.

Use This Tool

1. For Leaders: Use to assess your team's followership courage profile.
2. For Followers: Complete it yourself as a self-assessment.
3. For Teams: Discuss results together what does "courageous followership" mean for us?
4. For Development: Create growth plans for followers who need more courage in specific areas.

How to Reflection Exercise

My strongest courage dimension is:

_____

My weakest courage dimension is:

_____

One way I will show more courageous followership this month is:

_____

Tool 13: The Autonomy Spectrum

Purpose

Productive leadership is not about control **or** freedom it's about finding the right balance between the two, depending on a follower's **competence, reliability, past performance, and the complexity of work**.

The **Autonomy Spectrum Tool** helps leaders decide how much control or empowerment to give each follower, and to adjust that level as people develop.

Framework: The Five Levels of Autonomy

1. **Total Control** : Leader makes all decisions; follower executes exactly as instructed.
   - *Best for*: Inexperienced followers, high-risk tasks, crises.
2. **Guided Direction** : Leader provides clear structure, but explains the "why" and checks progress frequently.
   - *Best for*: Developing followers, new processes.
3. **Collaborative Involvement** : Leader and follower make decisions together; accountability is shared.
   - *Best for*: Medium competence, medium-risk tasks.
4. **Delegated Empowerment** : Follower decides and executes; leader monitors outcomes.
   - *Best for*: High-competence followers, routine or specialized work.
5. **Full Empowerment** : Follower has complete authority; leader trusts fully.
- *Best for*: Senior, highly reliable followers; long-term strategy roles.

PART 5 - TOOLS FOR PRODUCTIVE LEADERSHIP

The Questionnaire

Instructions: For each follower, consider the statements below. Rate on a scale of **1–5**:

1 = Strongly Disagree   2 = Disagree   3 = Neutral   4 = Agree   5 = Strongly Agree

1. This follower consistently delivers results without supervision. [1–5]
2. This follower can be trusted with sensitive or high-stakes tasks. [1–5]
3. This follower makes sound decisions aligned with organizational values. [1–5]
4. This follower proactively identifies and solves problems. [1–5]
5. This follower coaches or supports others in the team. [1–5]

Scoring:

- 5–10 → Level 1–2: Needs control and guidance.
- 11–15 → Level 3: Suitable for collaborative involvement.
- 16–20 → Level 4: Ready for delegated empowerment.
- 21–25 → Level 5: Ready for full empowerment.

How to Interpret

- **Low Scores (5–10):** This follower needs structure and support use Directive or Coaching styles.
- **Medium Scores (11–15):** Share decisions, involve them in choices use Democratic or Affiliative styles.
- **High Scores (16–25):** Empower them use Delegative or Visionary styles.

How to Use This Tool

- **Individual Development:** Use results to decide how much autonomy to grant each follower.
- **Performance Reviews:** Discuss autonomy with followers show them how trust grows with reliability.

- **Leadership Flexibility:** Adjust autonomy as competence and reliability evolve.
- **Team Culture:** Promote autonomy as both a privilege and responsibility.

Reflection Exercise

One follower I currently over-control is:

___

One follower I could empower more is:

___

A practical step I will take this month to adjust autonomy is:

___

Tool 14: VUCA–VUCA Prime Lens

Purpose

We live in a world defined by **VUCA, Volatility, Uncertainty, Complexity, Ambiguity**. These forces can overwhelm leaders and paralyze organizations.

The **VUCA–VUCA Prime Lens** helps leaders diagnose which element of VUCA dominates their situation, and apply the matching **VUCA Prime** response: **Vision, Understanding, Clarity, Agility.**

Framework

VUCA Challenge	Definition	Example	Leadership Response (VUCA Prime)
Volatility	Rapid, unpredictable change in environment or market.	Oil price shocks, pandemic lockdowns.	**Vision** – Provide clear direction and stability in turbulent times.
Uncertainty	Lack of predictability or reliable information.	Regulatory changes, election outcomes.	**Understanding** – Gather data, listen to multiple perspectives, seek patterns.
Complexity	Many interconnected variables and moving parts.	Global supply chain disruptions.	**Clarity** – Simplify processes, define roles, reduce noise.
Ambiguity	Situations with no clear answers or precedents.	Emerging technologies (AI, blockchain).	**Agility** – Experiment, adapt quickly, stay flexible.

PART 5 - TOOLS FOR PRODUCTIVE LEADERSHIP

The Questionnaire

Instructions: For your current situation, rate each statement on a scale of **1–5**: 1 = Strongly Disagree   2 = Disagree   3 = Neutral   4 = Agree   5 = Strongly Agree

- **Volatility**
  1. Market or environmental conditions are changing rapidly. [1–5]
  2. These changes are outside our control and affect us directly. [1–5]
- **Uncertainty**
  1. There is a lack of reliable information to guide decisions. [1–5]
  2. Outcomes are unpredictable despite planning. [1–5]
- **Complexity**
  1. There are multiple interdependencies making decisions difficult. [1–5]
  2. Many stakeholders are involved, increasing coordination challenges. [1–5]
- **Ambiguity**
  1. We are dealing with situations we have never faced before. [1–5]
  2. There is no clear precedent or "right answer" to follow. [1–5]

Scoring

- Add totals for each dimension (Volatility = Q1–2, Uncertainty = Q3–4, etc.).
- The highest scoring dimension = your **dominant VUCA challenge**.
- Apply the **matching VUCA Prime response** to counter it.

How to Interpret

- **Volatility High → Vision Needed**: Set long-term direction to calm turbulence.
- **Uncertainty High → Understanding Needed**: Expand sensing, gather insights, stay curious.
- **Complexity High → Clarity Needed**: Simplify and focus; don't overwhelm with detail.
- **Ambiguity High → Agility Needed**: Prototype, experiment, and stay adaptive.

How to Use This Tool

1. Complete the questionnaire for your current team/project.
2. Identify your dominant VUCA challenge.
3. Apply the matching VUCA Prime response.
4. Reassess regularly VUCA dimensions can shift rapidly.

Reflection Exercise

My current VUCA challenge is:

_____

The VUCA Prime response I need to strengthen is:

_____

One practical action I will take this month is:

_____

Tool 15: Change Leadership Roadmap

Purpose

Change is inevitable, but transformation succeeds only when leaders **guide people through the process**. The **Change Leadership Roadmap** provides leaders with a clear framework to:

1. Diagnose whether change is possible, and
2. Lead it step-by-step with proven practices.

Framework

Part 1: The Change Formula

Change occurs when: $D \times V \times F > R$

- **D = Dissatisfaction with the current state**
- **V = Vision of the future**
- **F = First steps**
- **R = Resistance to change**

If any one of D, V, or F is missing, resistance will win.

Part 2: Kotter's 8 Steps of Leading Change

1. **Create Urgency** : Make people dissatisfied with the status quo.
2. **Build a Guiding Coalition** : Form a powerful team to lead the change.
3. **Develop Vision and Strategy** : Paint a clear picture of the future.
4. **Communicate the Vision** : Share it repeatedly, through multiple channels.
5. **Empower Broad Action** : Remove obstacles and enable ownership.
6. **Generate Short-Term Wins** : Show quick results to build momentum.
7. **Consolidate Gains** – Build on early wins to tackle bigger challenges.
8. **Anchor Change in Culture** : Make it part of "how we do things here."

PART 5 - TOOLS FOR PRODUCTIVE LEADERSHIP

The Questionnaire

Instructions: For your current change initiative, rate each statement on a scale of **1–5**:

1 = Strongly Disagree   2 = Disagree   3 = Neutral   4 = Agree   5 = Strongly Agree

- **Dissatisfaction:** People feel the need for change. [1–5]
- **Vision:** A clear and compelling vision has been communicated. [1–5]
- **First Steps:** Concrete actions are underway to move forward. [1–5]
- **Resistance:** There is strong resistance from individuals or groups. [1–5]

If **D x V x F ≤ R**, your initiative is at risk.

How to Interpret

- **High Dissatisfaction but Weak Vision** → People know there's a problem, but don't see the solution.
- **Strong Vision but Weak First Steps** → People get inspired but lose faith when action lags.
- **Good Start but High Resistance** → Focus on communication and stakeholder engagement.
- **All Three Strong (D, V, F) > Resistance** → You're ready to accelerate through Kotter's 8 Steps.

How to Use This Tool

1. Diagnose your current state with the Change Formula.
2. Apply Kotter's 8 Steps sequentially, checking which step you're missing.
3. Share the roadmap with your leadership team to align on responsibilities.
4. Use it as a checklist during major initiatives (mergers, restructuring, digital transformation, culture shifts).

Reflection Exercise

My biggest source of dissatisfaction driving change is
_____

The most inspiring part of our vision is:
_____

The first step we must take immediately is
_____

The greatest source of resistance we face is
_____

Tool 16: Leadership Productivity Scorecard

Purpose

Productive leadership is not about working harder, but about creating systems that sustain results. The **Leadership Productivity Scorecard** gives leaders a structured way to measure their effectiveness across four dimensions of the **Balanced Scorecard**:

1. **Financial Impact**
2. **Customer & Stakeholder Value**
3. **Operational Excellence**
4. **Learning & Growth**

This tool turns leadership from abstract qualities into **measurable performance**.

Framework

Dimension	Definition	Example Leadership KPIs
Financial	How leadership decisions drive financial outcomes.	Revenue growth, cost savings, ROI of initiatives.
Customer & Stakeholder	How leadership impacts customers, clients, or stakeholders.	Net Promoter Score (NPS), stakeholder satisfaction, retention.
Operational Excellence	How leadership improves efficiency and processes.	Project delivery on time/on budget, compliance scores, process improvements.
Learning & Growth	How leadership develops people and culture.	% of team with development plans, training hours, employee engagement scores.

PART 5 - TOOLS FOR PRODUCTIVE LEADERSHIP

The Questionnaire

Instructions: For each dimension, rate yourself on a scale of **1–5**: 1 = Very Weak 2 = Weak   3 = Moderate   4 = Strong   5 = Very Strong

Financial Impact

1. My leadership decisions consistently improve financial performance. [1–5]
2. I balance short-term gains with long-term sustainability. [1–5]

Customer & Stakeholder Value

1. I consider the impact of my decisions on customers and stakeholders. [1–5]
2. I actively track and respond to customer/stakeholder feedback. [1–5]

Operational Excellence

1. I ensure that processes and projects are delivered on time and budget. [1–5]
2. I establish systems to reduce errors, risks, and inefficiencies. [1–5]

Learning & Growth

1. I invest in developing my team's skills and careers. [1–5]
2. I create a culture of continuous improvement and learning. [1–5]

Scoring

1. Add your scores for each dimension (max 10 per category).
2. Total possible score = 40.

Interpretation:

- **35–40 (Excellent):** You are leading with strong systemic productivity.
- **25–34 (Solid):** Good leadership foundation, with room for growth in one or two areas.
- **15–24 (Needs Attention):** Productivity risks are emerging — strengthen weak categories.
- **Below 15:** Leadership system is fragile — urgent redesign needed.

How to Interpret

- A leader strong in **Financial & Operations**, but weak in **Learning & Growth**, may get short-term wins but risk burnout or turnover.
- A leader strong in **Learning & Growth**, but weak in **Financial**, may inspire but fail to deliver results.
- True productivity comes from **balanced strength** across all four dimensions.

How to Use This Tool

1. Complete the scorecard quarterly as a self-assessment.
2. Compare results with feedback from your team or board.
3. Set measurable improvement goals in weak dimensions.
4. Integrate into performance reviews and leadership development plans.

Reflection Exercise

My strongest productivity dimension is:

___

My weakest productivity dimension is:

___

One concrete step I will take to improve this dimension is:

___

Tool 17: Productive Leadership Development Plan

Purpose

Leadership is not a destination it's a continuous journey. Productive leaders don't only plan for the business; they also design structured plans for **their own growth** and for the development of their teams.

The **Productive Leadership Development Plan** helps leaders commit to building new competencies, expanding their influence, and creating a sustainable legacy.

Framework

The plan focuses on four development dimensions:

1. **Self-Mastery** – Building awareness, resilience, and balance.
2. **Leadership Competencies** – Skills in strategy, influence, communication, decision-making.
3. **Team Development** – Investing in people's growth and succession.
4. **Impact & Legacy** – Expanding contribution to organization, industry, and society.

Development Plan Template

Dimension	Goal (SMART)	Development Activities	Resources	Timeline	Measure of Success
Self-Mastery	e.g., Improve stress management	Daily journaling, mindfulness	App, coach	3 months	Lower stress score
Leadership Competence	e.g., Improve communication	Public speaking course	Online course	6 months	Deliver 3 external speeches

PART 5 - TOOLS FOR PRODUCTIVE LEADERSHIP

Team Development	e.g., Build future leaders	Assign stretch projects	Mentorship, LinkedIn Learning	Ongoing	3 team members promoted
Impact & Legacy	e.g., Expand influence	Publish thought leadership	Writing, conferences	12 months	2 articles published

How to Complete the Tool

1. Identify **1–2 goals per dimension** (SMART: Specific, Measurable, Achievable, Relevant, Time-bound).
2. Choose development activities (courses, coaching, books, projects).
3. Allocate resources (budget, time, mentors, technology).
4. Set a timeline and measures of success.
5. Review quarterly and adjust.

How to Use This Tool

- **For Leaders:** Complete your own plan and share with your mentor or coach.
- **For Teams:** Create individual development plans for all direct reports.
- **For Organizations:** Integrate into performance management and talent development systems.
- **For Legacy:** Track growth over years — leadership maturity is built through consistent, planned investment.

Reflection Exercise

- One area I most want to grow as a leader is: _____
- A resource I will use to support this growth is: _____
- The impact I want this growth to have on my team/organization is: _____

By now, you have worked through a complete **Productive Leadership Toolkit**. These 17 tools were designed to:

- Translate leadership concepts into **daily practice**.

- Help you assess yourself as a leader, understand your followers, and analyze situations.
- Provide adaptable frameworks for decision-making, communication, and growth.
- Build not only leaders, but also leadership systems that endure.

The key takeaway is this: **tools are not the destination they are enablers.** They only create impact when you use them consistently, with your team, linked to action.

As you move forward, don't try to master all 17 tools at once. Select one or two that are most relevant to your current context, apply them, and reflect on the results. Over time, integrate more into your practice until you have a **personalized leadership operating system**.

Productive leadership is not luck. It is design. And with these tools, you now have the design instruments to lead with clarity, adaptability, and purpose in any situation, with any team.

CONCLUSION

The Keys to Productive Leadership

"Leadership is not who you are, but what happens between leaders, followers, and situations and the key to productivity is mastering that process."

ALI KASA

Leadership has been studied for centuries. Thousands of books, millions of articles, and countless training programs exist. Yet the confusion remains: What truly makes leadership work?

This book has sought to simplify the answer: leadership is a process a dynamic interplay of leader, followers, and situation, anchored in purpose and measured by outcomes. Productive leadership is not about titles, charisma, or personality; it is about creating results through alignment, adaptability, and accountability.

The Journey We Took

- **Part 1: Understanding Leadership**

    We explored what leadership really is, traced key theories, and challenged the myths that leaders are simply born with fixed styles. We reframed leadership as a process, not a position.

- **Part 2: Focus on the Leader**

    We examined the leader's role: power, values, vision, traits, behaviors, energy, influence, and levels of leadership. Leaders must know themselves, grow themselves, and flex their styles.

- **Part 3: Focus on Followers**

    We emphasized that leadership is half about followers. Their competence, commitment, trust, and reliability shape the quality of leadership.

CONCLUSION

Courageous followership, readiness, and shared purpose transform "employees" into true partners.

- **Part 4: Focus on the Situation**

  We looked at how contexts stable or volatile, simple or complex demand different approaches. From VUCA challenges to engineered situations and leading change, leaders must diagnose reality before deciding how to act.

- **Part 5: Tools for Productive Leadership**

  Finally, we provided practical instruments: the Leadership Canvas, Situational Matrix, Style–Situation Matching Tool, Follower Readiness Matrix, Autonomy Spectrum, VUCA Prime Framework, Change Formula & Kotter's Steps, and the Leadership Scorecard. These tools form a leadership operating system that makes the process repeatable, measurable, and teachable.

The Ten Keys of Productive Leadership

Throughout, we distilled everything into Ten Keys:

1. Leadership is a process, not a position.
2. Purpose anchors everything.
3. Leaders must master self-awareness and adaptability.
4. Followers are equal partners in leadership.
5. Situations must be diagnosed, not assumed.
6. Influence comes from trust, not authority.
7. Energy sets the climate leaders create the weather.
8. Systems and tools sustain productivity.
9. Leadership must be measured, not left to chance.
10. Productive leaders engineer alignment between leader, followers, and situation.

The Call to Action

The world does not need more leaders in title. It needs more leaders in practice. Leaders who:

- Inspire with purpose,
- Adapt their style,
- Empower their followers,
- Engineer their situations, and
- Measure their impact.

The challenge for you, the reader, is simple: Don't just read this book. Use it.

- Fill out the canvas.
- Map your followers.
- Match your style to situations.
- Measure yourself with the scorecard.
- Most of all, revisit your purpose and commit to leading productively.

Leadership will never be easy, but it can be productive. If you remember nothing else from this book, remember this:

Leadership is what happens between leaders, followers, and situations and your role is to align them around a shared purpose with clarity, adaptability, and accountability.

That is the essence. That is the system. That is the key.

FINAL WORD FROM THE AUTHOR

I believe, with all my heart, that everyone is a leader. Leadership does not begin with a title, a position, or a corner office. It begins with the one person you will lead for your entire life yourself.

Self-management is the first act of leadership. How you manage your energy, your values, your time, and your focus will determine whether you are capable of leading others. If you cannot lead yourself with discipline and purpose, you will not inspire others to trust you with their future.

But leadership does not stop at self-mastery. It culminates in interaction in what happens between leaders, followers, and situations. Every interaction is a chance to build trust, align around purpose, and move closer to shared outcomes. Leadership is not a solo performance; it is a process created together with others.

That is why I believe in productive leadership. Leadership that is not measured by power or personality, but by results. Leadership that creates outcomes by aligning the leader, the followers, and the situation around a shared purpose. Leadership that is disciplined, accountable, and sustainable.

This book has given you frameworks, tools, and stories to practice productive leadership. But tools are only as powerful as the hands that use them. The true test is not what you know, but how you apply it to create results that matter for your organization, your people, and your purpose.

So wherever you are in your journey whether you are a CEO shaping a company, a manager guiding a team, or an individual leading your own life remember this: you already hold the keys to productive leadership.

Use them wisely. Share them generously. Refine them daily. And above all, let your leadership serve a greater purpose.

Go lead productively.
— Ali Kasa

EPILOGUE
THE LEGACY OF LEADERSHIP

Leadership is not a position we hold it is a space we create. It is the invisible bridge between purpose and people, between vision and reality. Long after the title fades, the systems evolve, and the leader moves on, what remains is the *impact* the culture, the trust, the habits, and the courage we leave behind.

Throughout this book, we have explored the mechanics of leadership the leader, the followers, and the situation and the tools that make the process productive. But the real essence of leadership lies beyond productivity; it lies in *continuity*. Productive leadership is not about how much you achieve in your lifetime, but how much continues to grow after you are gone.

Every truly great leader becomes invisible in success. Their influence lives in the people they develop, the standards they set, and the systems they design. The goal of productive leadership is not control it is *creation*. It is the art of building something that can thrive without you.

Legacy is not measured in monuments or metrics. It is written in the stories people tell when you are no longer in the room. It is in the mentee who becomes a mentor, in the culture that upholds integrity without supervision, in the team that solves problems with shared purpose. It is in the quiet strength of a follower who once needed guidance and now leads others with clarity and care.

In the end, leadership comes full circle. You begin by learning to lead yourself mastering values, vision, and behavior. Then, you learn to lead others building trust, influence, and collaboration. Finally, you learn to lead *beyond yourself* creating systems, cultures, and successors who carry the flame forward.

If this book leaves you with one message, let it be this: leadership is not about being followed; it is about making others capable of leading. It is about turning

THE LEGACY OF LEADERSHIP

potential into purpose, and purpose into performance. It is about leaving every person, every team, and every system stronger than you found it.

May your leadership journey be guided by clarity, sustained by purpose, and remembered not for the position you held, but for the possibilities you created.

Because true leadership does not end it multiplies.

— Ali Kasa - *Author, Entrepreneur, Educator & Potential Optimiser*

AFTERWORD & RESOURCES

Leadership is not learned once; it is lived daily. The more we practice it, the more we realize that productive leadership is not about authority or control it's about clarity, contribution, and continuity.

If this book has sparked new thoughts, challenged your assumptions, or reignited your sense of purpose, then your leadership journey is just beginning. My hope is that you'll take these ideas into your organizations, your teams, and your communities and become part of a new global movement of *Productive Leaders*: individuals committed to leading with purpose, building with integrity, and leaving lasting impact.

Join the Movement: The Productive Leader Initiative

Be part of a growing network of CEOs, founders, educators, and professionals dedicated to raising the standards of leadership worldwide. Together, we'll share ideas, tools, and real stories of transformation.

Join at: www.alikasa.me/productiveleader

Follow the hashtag: #ProductiveLeader #LeadershipByDesign

ACKNOWLEDGMENTS

This book would not have been possible without the guidance, inspiration, and support of many people who shaped my journey.

First, I thank my teachers and mentors, who planted the seeds of curiosity and discipline in me. Their wisdom, advice, and sometimes tough lessons continue to guide my path as both a student and a practitioner of leadership.

I am grateful to the leaders and colleagues I have worked with over the years, especially my teams. Your trust, commitment, and even your challenges have sharpened me. Every success I have had is because of the people who chose to walk beside me.

To my team today, thank you for your dedication and the countless hours spent building, improving, and challenging what leadership looks like in practice. This book is shaped by the reality we face together daily.

To my family, whose love, patience, and encouragement have carried me through every high and low you are my foundation. Without your support, none of this work would matter.

And finally, to the readers of this book: you are now part of this journey. My hope is that these pages help you unlock your own potential and the potential of those you lead.

Thank you all for being part of my leadership story.— Ali Kasa

RECOMMENDED READING & INSPIRATION

To continue your leadership growth journey, explore these timeless works that complement the ideas in this book:

- *The 7 Habits of Highly Effective People* – Stephen R. Covey
- *Leaders Eat Last* – Simon Sinek
- *Good to Great* – Jim Collins
- *Drive: The Surprising Truth About What Motivates Us* – Daniel Pink
- *The Fifth Discipline* – Peter Senge
- *Atomic Habits* – James Clear
- *The Infinite Game* – Simon Sinek

BOOKS BY ALI KASA

Ali Kasa is the author of a growing series of practical leadership and life design titles that empower individuals and organizations to unleash their potential. Explore the complete collection:

1. **Keys to High-Impact Corporate Governance**
2. **Keys to Successful Business Succession**
3. **Keys to Productive Succession Planning**
4. **Lean Entrepreneur's Manual**
5. **Life Architect's Manual**
6. **Freedom, by Design: The Hard Choices to Live Free**

All titles are available in eBook, print, hardcover, and audiobook formats on Amazon, Lulu, IngramSpark, and leading online retailers.

CONNECT WITH ALI KASA

Let's stay connected and continue building a world of productive, purpose-driven leaders:

Website: www.alikasa.me

LinkedIn: https://www.linkedin.com/in/thealikasa/

Facebook: facebook.com/alikasa.official

Instagram: instagram.com/alikasa.official

TikTok: tiktok.com/@thealikasa

Podcast: *Potential by Design* — available on Spotify, Apple Podcasts, and Google Podcasts

For speaking engagements, interviews, or corporate programs, please visit: **www.alikasa.me/speaking**

FINAL WORD

The world doesn't need more leaders it needs more *productive* ones. Leaders who create clarity, build capacity, and measure success not by the power they hold but by the progress they enable.

The journey ahead is not about becoming someone else; it's about becoming the best version of yourself intentionally, courageously, and consistently. Together, let's build a world led by purpose, guided by values, and measured by impact.